Small Pleasures

So often, we exhaust ourselves and the planet in a search for very large pleasures, while all around us lies a wealth of small pleasures, which – if only we paid more attention – could daily bring us solace and joy at little cost and effort. But we need some encouragement to focus our gaze. This is a book to guide us to the best of life's small pleasures: everything from the distinctive delight of holding a child's hand to the enjoyment of disagreeing with someone or the joy of the evening sky; an intriguing, evocative mix of small pleasures that will heighten our senses and return us to the world with new-found excitement and enthusiasm.

Published in 2016 by The School of Life
70 Marchmont Street, London WC1N 1AB
Copyright © The School of Life 2016
Designed and typeset by FLOK, Berlin
Printed in Latvia by Livonia Print

A proportion of this book has appeared online at thebookoflife.org.

Every effort has been made to contact the copyright holders of the material
reproduced in this book. If any have been inadvertently overlooked,
the publisher will be pleased to make restitution at the earliest opportunity.

www.theschooloflife.com

ISBN 978-0-9935387-3-5

Small
Pleasures

Contents

Preface

What This Book Is For

There are many little things that charm us – a favourite old jumper, whispering in the dark or the taste of a fig – when we happen to have the time to notice. They're the small pleasures of everyday life. This book looks at 52 of them in detail, perhaps one for every week of the year. Usually, small pleasures are not widely celebrated or even much talked about. Every chapter puts one such moment of enjoyment under a kind of magnifying glass to find out what's really going on in it and why it touches and moves us and makes us smile. It's a search for the bigger meaning secretly lurking in everything we find nice. Small pleasures turn out not to be small at all: they are points of access to the great themes of our lives.

It can at first sound slightly strange to say that we don't automatically and naturally know how to enjoy ourselves. But the pursuit of pleasure is a skill which we need to learn: it's something that we can get better at. And small pleasures are the things to start with.

Not all the small pleasures in your life will be listed here, of course. We're seeking to build a philosophy of appreciation that encourages us to explore more deeply – and get more out of – the many sources of happiness that are currently a bit neglected. Small pleasures, we believe, are pleasures whose true importance is not yet properly understood. This book is a step in a wider cultural project – to move these small pleasures from the margins closer to the centre of our collective consciousness and our lives.

1
The Fish Shop

The fishmonger's window display is alluring, yet one doesn't normally go in. But when one does, one wonders why one doesn't visit more often.

Waiting to be served, one is struck by the beauty and strangeness of the fish and sea creatures on offer on the beds of ice: the oyster that somehow generates its own home, rocky on the outside, suggestively smooth and polished within. For a moment one contemplates the destiny of the sole, one of whose eyes has to migrate round its head on the path to maturity, and the monkfish, whose huge, toothy mouth and puny body are repellent to look at but whose flesh is delicious when roasted and drizzled with olive oil.

They seem so alien. But – in a universe composed almost entirely of gas and rock circulating in the endless nothingness of space – we are their cousins, with whom we briefly cohabit the surface zones of earth. In the recent history of the cosmos, we shared common ancestors, whose progeny became diversely the octopus, the sea bream or evolved gradually into solicitors, psychotherapists and graphic designers.

Imagine spending this thing called life embodied in a lobster, encountering the world through its tiny peppercorn eyes, which offer a field of vision much wider but less focused than ours. There would have been the momentous day one dug a burrow beneath a basalt rock in the soft mud of the sea floor in Fidden Bay, off the Isle of Mull. Then there would have been the drama of shedding our exoskeleton. We would have had to master the laborious process of reproduction, when the male has to pierce the female's stomach to deposit his spermatophores. Finally there was the catastrophic curiosity that two days ago tempted us into a lobster pot.

The fish shop isn't simply a place to pick up calamari rings or some cod steaks, it is also a place of re-enchantment. We suffer a fatally easy tendency to become jaded. Things that are familiar lose their power to entice the imagination. Then, looking into the eye of a mullet, or contemplating the internal architecture of a skate fin, one is reconnected with the elegant and bizarre inventiveness of nature. We've been too hasty; we've overlooked almost everything. The world is full of fascination; there is so much to be explored. And we have been led to this renewed appetite by the head of a fish.

Each item has been gathered from the chambers of the sea, distant rivers, or prised from submerged rocks. The speckled trout were reared in a former gravel pit in Lincolnshire. The mackerel were caught by a trawler on the Dogger Bank and landed at Peterhead. The sea bass were hauled onto the cobbled pier at Crail and speeded in a refrigerated van down the M90 and the A1(M) with a brief halt in the HGV parking lot at Wetherby Service Station.

And here they all are cleansed, gutted, chilled and artfully arranged. Nature has been civilised and made attractive by ice, metal, glass, tiles, slabs of marble and by constant cold water and the sharpest knives. The fish shop hints at an ideal that we would like perhaps to pursue more broadly: the sense that trouble has been rinsed away, and the desirable good bit will be delivered into your life neatly wrapped in delicately glazed white paper.

Visiting the fishmonger leads one to sketch little plans of moral reform: in another, slightly better, life, one would go there all the time. We'd become adept at preparing certain dishes. Being here, one makes fleeting, initial contact with a latent self who poaches salmon, tosses a lobster salad, drizzles olive oil and whose friends come round for bouillabaisse. There is a potential future version of oneself – who starts to come to life in the fishmonger – who lives on light, nutritious fishy meals and whose brain is bathed in their sympathetic briny fluids. Life as a whole will remain radically imperfect, one knows, but if one took slightly more care around eating, even if lots of bits of one's life were bad, if one could come in here and get some sole wrapped up by the man in the blue apron and go home, and take the art of living more seriously, then one would be closer to being the person one should always have been. The fish shop pleasure originates in very small points of departure – the smell of the salt and water, the frigid air wafting from the beds of ice, the silvery skin of an Atlantic salmon – and grows into a large idea: respect for civilisations that have more time for things that are simultaneously delightful and wholesome.

2

Small Islands

As the plane makes its gradual descent, you see much of the island from your window: the cliffs at one end, the long golden curve of a remote beach, olive groves, an isolated village, a patch of woodland, the ferry wharf constructed in the 1970s, the whitewashed air traffic control tower. There's just one carousel at the terminal. People seem to know each other. It's only a short ride in the hired car into the small main town. You drive past the shopping centre, the villa with the old tree in front, the primary school, the restaurant that specialises in seafood, the town hall ... And there's a strange, instinctive feeling of wanting to live here. You won't really, in all probability, for a lot of reasons big and small. But the thought of being happy here is saying something important – which deserves to be decoded and which might not ultimately involve plans for relocation.

Small islands tap into the pleasing sense of control that comes with a reduced, more manageable scale. It's why Legoland is a great tourist attraction and why the Poppenhuis – a doll's house – is the most popular exhibit in Amsterdam's majestic Rijksmuseum. When the world gets smaller, we get larger – and feel less vulnerable, more competent. A small island offers to fulfil the childhood dream of adult existence. At last we will be big people, like the adults we then admired and felt so reassured by.

You can easily drive out to the highest point of the island – a modest climb from the half-deserted car park. From there you can see pretty much the whole place: the bay where it's great to swim, then, a bit further round the coast, the harbour with the town clustering round it; in the distance there's the spire of the monastery. The small island has obvious boundaries you can see. You can walk right round the coast road in a few hours. Even when you are in the middle of the town you can catch sight of the surrounding hills, or glimpse the bay, at the end of various streets.

It's an attractive contrast to the mostly unbounded issues we have to deal with in the rest of existence: one of the big causes of stress is that we often face problems that can't be solved in any reasonable period of time or indeed solved at all. It's going to take five more years until we're ready to start the job we really want. That big project at work will take another 24 months before it shows any signs of real progress. The annoying colleague is a daily challenge, with no end in sight. Even now, deep in adulthood, your sibling or parent remains an ongoing source of frustration. You've just had the same argument for the twentieth time with your partner; it always ends in apologies, but a real advance is elusive. Your child has again damaged the sofa. In other words, our longing for control and completion is constantly being frustrated.

It's to this corrosive tendency that the island seems to offer a contrastive antidote: limited, defined, contained – and you can get anywhere in a shortish drive.

We easily forget how much love is connected to being able to look after something. We turn inwards and become what is called selfish when the social problems feel too vast and intractable and our own efforts start to look puny and pointless. The great metropolitan centres are too big to love. They constantly force us to admit that we are nothing. The small island is so pleasing because it raises the vision of another kind of world, in which public effort and generosity feel logical and productive. The gap between tidying one's bedroom and tidying the little world of the island is not so daunting.

An island foregrounds the particular rather than the general (to put it in a rather abstract way, initially). It turns out there's pretty much only one of everything. There's one high school, one fancy restaurant, one cinema, one good place to buy shellfish, one airport, one bookshop, one museum, one nightclub, the beach where you swim on hot days, the mountain where it's always cool. You go back to the same place again and again – because there isn't always another competing for your attention. Things become familiar, relationships become intimate.

Of course, the reality of any particular small island won't be exactly like this, flaws will always arise. But the feeling of pleasure we experience on arrival is partly the work of the imagination. In fact, the pleasure of the small island rests on qualities that (once we have learned to recognise them) can be found closer to home. A small island is not just a place on the map; it's a psychological destination, a model of simplifying your life and making do with what is immediately to hand. You may not even have to take a plane or a boat to get there.

3

Stars

It's strange to see there are so many of them, though in some detached part of our brains we know there are trillions of trillions of them. But we forget to look. We keep meaning to, but it might only be once or twice a year we find ourselves looking up on a dark night at our own sliver of the universe.

When we do, we feel ourselves pleasantly diminished by the majesty of what we contemplate. As we renew our connection with immensity, we're humbled without being humiliated. It's not just us, personally and individually, who are diminished in comparison. The things that trouble and bother us seem smaller as well.

The sight of the stars – perhaps glimpsed above a suburban railway station coming home late after an extended crisis in the office, or from a bedroom window on a sleepless night – presents us with a direct, sensory impression of the magnitude of the cosmos. Without knowing the exact details, we're powerfully aware that their light has been beaming down changelessly through recorded history, that our great-grandparents must have, from time to time, looked on just the same pattern of tiny lights. They look so densely packed and yet we grasp that they are in fact separated by astonishing gulfs of empty nothingness; that around them circle unknown worlds – lifeless, maybe, or perhaps teeming with alien vitality and harbouring dramas of incomprehensible splendour and tragedy about which we will never know anything, though perhaps in a hundred or a thousand generations our descendants will be at home even there. It is sublime because we are drawn entirely out of the normal course of our daily concerns and our thoughts are directed to matters in which we have no personal stake whatever. Our private lives fall into the background, which is a contrastive relief to the normal state of anxious preoccupation with the local and the immediate.

We're taught that interest in the stars is scientific, but it should be humanistic. If a child gets excited by the stars, parents feel that they should undertake a visit to a planetarium and make a stab at explaining thermonuclear fusion, gravity, the speed of light, red giants, white dwarfs and black holes. The presiding assumption is that an interest in the stars must be directed towards a knowledge of astrophysics.

But very few of us will become science professionals. We can afford to be impressionistic because it never will really matter whether we can remember much of the detail. We're amateurs and we need something else. The stars matter in our lives because they offer a consoling encounter with grandeur, because they invite a helpful perspective on the brevity and littleness of human existence. Why don't we make more of this natural resource and plug ourselves more frequently into the Milky Way and renew this helpful pleasure?

It's an issue that crops up so often around small pleasures. There's an accidental randomness to our encounters with them. We leave it to chance. Ideally we'd schedule more appointments. We'd put it in the diary: meeting with the stars, Tuesday (a moonless night, cloud cover predicted to be 20 per cent) 9.15 pm – a walk after dinner.

Our collective model of a good life tends to focus on career progress and financial management. We don't typically weigh up whether a person went to the fish shop a lot, paid a lot of attention to islands or looked very much at the stars. Yet, in fact, the regular appreciation of these and related small pleasures makes a major contribution to the elusive but crucially important notion of the quality of existence. Such pleasures can be termed small because they don't usually have big, immediate, dramatic consequences. We don't crave them; they come to us fairly quietly and are easily missed against a background of distractions and preoccupations. We don't have to do anything about them. And so, lovely though they are, they easily slip out of view.

One of the big tasks of civilisation is to teach us how to better enjoy life. The Romantic assumption is that we know intuitively and all we need is greater freedom to follow our instincts. The Classical picture is that a pleasant life is, in fact, a deliberate accomplishment. It's a rational achievement that builds on the careful examination of experience and involves deliberate strategies to guide us more reliably to the things that truly please us.

4
Grandmothers

Naturally, the details of personal experience vary enormously, but there's a charming ideal of what a grandmother is that we can imagine or piece together from fragments of benign memories.

Perhaps when you were a child, when your parents and siblings were away for some reason, you spent a couple of days on your own just with her at her house. You were 6, you helped in the kitchen, there was a special smell in the cupboard where she kept the plates and a strange set of dark green glasses; she had a funny toaster with a large red lever and a special little fat knife only for butter. She took you to a farm in her little car and you fed a carrot to a goat and she told you about a pet pig she had when she lived in the country as a child. She cut up an apple in a special way, removing the whole peel in one wonderful long spiral. And she gave you a thin mint chocolate and she laughed when you didn't really like it. But she didn't mind. She gave you supper on a tray and let you watch television, sitting on her big sofa.

There was a wooden chest with her special things: some old coins, a fan made of ivory, a tiny pencil made of gold, a photo of her at a beach and a slightly sinister one in which she's standing next to a man in soldier's uniform which she says was taken 'during the war'. You were being introduced to an outside world bigger than your parents'. It was alien, but because of her involvement, it is still one you are connected to.

A grandmother can function as what the British psycho-analyst Donald Winnicott called a transitional object. A transitional object (like a favourite blanket or an increasingly grubby knitted rabbit) stands for home, but it can also accompany the child in its early forays into the wider world. It provides an extended psychological lifeline back to maternal love and security. In its presence the child feels emotionally safe and can therefore risk experimenting with things that are at first a little frightening or alien. The grandmother is kind and gentle, and in her reassuring presence the child can start to encounter ideas that are potentially distressing: the fact that the world is very big, with a huge, complex past and filled with strangers.

There is a sweet alliance of the elderly grandmother (who is gradually becoming weaker) and the young grandchild (who is slowly becoming stronger). But at the moment, from opposite ends of the spectrum, they both understand frailty quite well. There's an open-ended tenderness in the grandmother's attitude. Her awareness of her own short tenure on life makes her feel the preciousness of mere existence. She'll probably die before the course of your adult life is established. She might not be able to talk about Minecraft or know how to make a spaceship out of Lego; she can't make an obstacle course round the sitting room out of cushions and upturned chairs. But she's very interested in whether you still like Toblerone and if you might be feeling a little bit cold. She may be the only person who simply wants you to be happy. She's good at being cosy. It's nice to snuggle up to her while she reads to you. She embodies a species of wisdom: the knowledge that achievement is in the long run overrated, that simply being comfortable sitting next to another person watching a gardening programme on television, or carefully watering a potted geranium in the company of a small person, can be deeply important.

Ironically, it is this pure kindness which is so irritating when you become a teenager. She's delighted – of course – if you win the long jump and will obligingly coo over your maths exam results. But you sense that she would be just as warm if you had two left feet and couldn't make any sense of algebra. Because her love is unconditional, it has the potentially maddening tendency to look right past some of your actual merits, which are the present focus of your own sense of who you are. She wants to hug you and tuck you in and do a jigsaw together.

She seems – in a way that will become awkward – to represent the opposite of sex. When she was 22 she was very different. She's actually been through every permutation of experience. But it doesn't seem that way when you are 13. Excitement doesn't touch her now. Inevitably – but quite wrongly – you feel she'd be shocked and upset to know of the inner complications of your growing imagination. You were still too young to realise that even though she likes patterned jumpers and takes care going down stairs, she's the same person who once spent a riotous summer shacked up with a drunken conceptual artist in West Berlin.

The parent is desperate that the child will grow up well; the lover wants to be understood; the friend wants a companion in adventure. The grandmother doesn't want anything from you, except your presence. It's a disconcerting innocence: the lack of calculation and an absence of desire. She doesn't appear to acknowledge any of the driving forces in your life. It's not actually because she never knew them but because they no longer particularly impress her terribly much. She's seen boys grow into lawyers and then judges, or A-grade students, doctors and then surgeons – and it doesn't amaze her because she's also seen these people have messy personal lives, decline physically, develop prostate issues and die suddenly. It means she focuses on now and can therefore seem boring: for example, her interest in mentioning that there used to be a dry-cleaners where there's now a health food shop; her habit of saying 'the' Facebook; her confusion at how her phone works.

The pleasure we take in the idea of the grandmother is a way of acknowledging how much we actually like tenderness. Ordinarily, relationships should learn a lesson in love from this slightly funny situation – the encounter between an elderly lady and a child. It doesn't look like a likely classroom where we can gain much of an education. But this is the true crucible of love – a topic which we are so invested in but around which we have so many failures. What we learn is how important modesty of ambition is. It's where we see how love can be so beneficially detached from expectation and from reciprocation. The grandmother never hopes to be understood by the child. It is enough to spend a nice day, without doing much: we saw a pony, had some milk, played a game of cards, tried doing a painting of a flower. Quite soon, the 6-year-old will start to think this is a ridiculous day. And it may take six decades before they relearn that it is the purpose and meaning of life.

The longing, embodied in the happy idea of the grandmother, is that we can learn this lesson a little better and a little sooner: that we will be able to decant a portion of this love-wisdom before too much of life is past.

The Friend Who Listens

Given how much we value friendship, it's strange that we're not so focused on one of its central pleasures: being listened to.

Few of us know how to do it, not because we are evil, but because no one has taught us how and – a related point – no one has listened to us. So we come to social life greedy to speak rather than listen, hungry to meet others, but reluctant to hear them. Friendship degenerates into a socialised egoism. Like most things, it's about education. Our civilisation is full of great books on how to speak – Cicero's *Orator* and Aristotle's *Rhetoric* were two of the greatest in the ancient world – but sadly no one has ever written a book called 'The Listener'. There is a range of things that the good listener is doing that makes it so nice to spend time in their company. Firstly: they egg us on. It's hard to know our own minds. Often, we're in the vicinity of something, but we don't quite close in on what's really bothering or exciting us. We hugely benefit from the encouragement to elaborate, to go into greater detail, to push a little further. We need someone who, rather than launch forth, will simply say those two magic words: go on ... You mention a sibling and they want to know a bit more. What was the relationship like in childhood? How has it changed over time? They're curious where our concerns and excitements come from. They ask things like: why did that particularly bother you? Why was that such a big thing for you? They keep our histories in mind, they might refer back to something we said before, and we feel they're building up a deeper base of engagement.

Secondly: they urge clarification. It's fatally easy to say vague things: we simply mention that something is lovely or terrible, nice or annoying. But we don't really explore why we feel this way. The friend who listens often has a productive, friendly suspicion of some of our own first statements and is after the deeper attitudes that are lurking in the background. They take things we say, like 'I'm fed up with my job' or 'My partner and I are having a lot of rows …', and help us to focus on what it really is about the job we don't like or what the rows are really about. They're bringing to listening an ambition to clarify the underlying issues. They don't just see conversation as the swapping of anecdotes. They are reconnecting the chat you're having over pizza with the philosophical ambitions of Socrates, whose dialogues are records of his attempts to help his fellow Athenians understand their own ideas and values.

Thirdly: they don't moralise. The good listener is acutely aware of how insane we all are. They know their own minds well enough not to be surprised or frightened about this. They're skilled at making occasional little positive sounds: strategic 'mmms' that delicately signal sympathy without intruding on what we're trying to say. They give the impression they recognise and accept our follies; they're reassuring us they're not going to shred our dignity. A big worry in a competitive world is that we feel we can't afford to be honest about how distressed we are. Saying one feels like a failure could mean being dropped. The good listener signals early and clearly that they don't see us in these terms. Our vulnerability is something they warm to rather than are appalled by.

Fourthly: they separate disagreement from criticism. There's a huge tendency to feel that being disagreed with is an expression of hostility. And obviously sometimes this is right. But a good listener makes it clear that they can really like you and, at the same time, think you are wrong. They make it plain that their liking for you isn't dependent on constant agreement. They are powerfully aware that a really lovely person could end up a bit muddled and in need of some gentle untangling.

When we're in the company of people who listen well, we experience a very powerful pleasure, but too often, we don't really realise what it is about what this person is doing that is so nice. By paying strategic attention to the pleasure, we can learn to magnify it and offer it to others, who will notice, heal – and repay the favour in turn. Listening deserves discovery as one of the keys to a good society.

6

Take-Off

Few seconds in life are as ecstatic as those in which a plane ascends to the sky. Looking out of a window from a machine standing stationary at the beginning of a runway, we face a vista of familiar proportions: a road, oil cylinders, grass and hotels with copper-tinted windows; the earth as we have always known it, where we make slow progress, even with the help of a car, where calf muscles and engines strain to reach the summit of hills, where, half a mile ahead or less, there is almost always a line of trees or buildings to restrict our view. Then, suddenly, accompanied by the controlled rage of the engines (with only a slight tremor from glasses in the galley), we rise fluently into the atmosphere and an immense horizon opens up across which we can wander without impediment. A journey which on earth would have taken an afternoon can be accomplished with an infinitesimal movement of the eye; we can cross Berkshire, glimpse Maidenhead, survey Bracknell and overtake every car on the M4.

There is psychological pleasure in this take-off too, for the swiftness of the plane's ascent is an exemplary symbol of transformation. The display of power can inspire us to imagine analogous, decisive shifts in our own lives; to imagine that we too might one day surge above much that had loomed over us.

The new vantage point lends order and logic to the landscape: roads curve to avoid hills; rivers trace paths to lakes; pylons lead from power stations to towns; streets, which from earth seemed laid out without thought, emerge as well-planned grids. The eye attempts to match what it can see with what it knows should be there, like trying to decipher a familiar book in a new language. The lights must be Newbury, the road the A34 as it leaves the M4. And to think that all along, hidden from our sight, our lives were this small: the world we live in but almost never see; the way we must appear to the hawk and to the gods.

The engines show none of the effort required to take us to this place. They hang in the inconceivable cold, patiently and invisibly powering the craft, their sole requests, painted on their inner flanks in red letters, that we do not walk on them and that we feed them 'Oil only: D50TFI-S4', a message for a forthcoming set of men in overalls, 4,000 miles away and still asleep.

There is not much talk about the clouds visible up here. No one thinks it remarkable that somewhere above an ocean we flew past a vast white candyfloss island which would have made a perfect seat for an angel or even God himself in a painting by Piero della Francesca. In the cabin, no one stands up to announce with requisite emphasis that, out of the window, we are flying over a cloud, a matter that would have detained Leonardo and Poussin, Claude and Constable.

Food that, if eaten in a kitchen, would have been banal or offensive, acquires a new taste and interest in the presence of clouds (like a picnic of bread and cheese that delights us when eaten on a clifftop above a pounding sea). With the in-flight tray, we make ourselves at home in this unhomely place: we appropriate the extraterrestrial landscape with the help of a chilled bread roll and a plastic tray of potato salad.

The clouds usher in tranquillity. Below us are enemies and colleagues, the sites of our terrors and our griefs, all of them now infinitesimal, scratches on the earth. We may know this old lesson in perspective well enough, but rarely does it seem as true as when we are pressed against the cold plane window, our beautiful purposeful machine a teacher of profound philosophy.

A Night Alone in a Hotel

You've been in the air for 12 hours. Now this anonymous box. It was your company's idea. You'd have a chance to sleep a little, then catch the next 11-hour flight, before heading straight into the conference.

You've been assigned a room at the top western corner of the building from which you can see one side of a terminal and a sequence of red and white lights that mark the end of a runway. Every minute, despite the best attempts of the glazing contractors, you hear the roar of an ascending jet, as hundreds of passengers, some perhaps holding their partners' hands, others sanguinely scanning *The Economist*, head out over the Straits of Singapore.

You're hungry and hunt out the room service menu. 'Pacific snapper, enhanced with lemon pepper seasoning atop a chunky mango relish.' The always dour 'Chef's soup of the day'. But perhaps, in the end, there's never a better alternative to the club sandwich, which you've never eaten (or even noticed) anywhere but in places like this.

There is a knock at the door 20 minutes later. It is a strange moment when two adults meet each other, one naked save for a complimentary dressing gown, the other (newly arrived in Singapore from the little village of Ujung Batu in Indonesia and sharing a room with four others near the sports stadium) sporting a black-and-white uniform with an apron and name badge. It is difficult to think of the ritual as entirely unremarkable, to say in a casually impatient voice, 'By the television, please,' while pretending to rearrange papers – though this capacity can be counted upon to evolve with more frequent attendance at global conferences.

You have dinner with Chloe Cho, formerly with CNBC, now working for Channel NewsAsia in Singapore. She updates you on the regional markets and Samsung's quarterly forecast. You wonder what Chloe's outside interests might be.

It's impossible to get to sleep. The prehistoric part of your mind, trained to listen for and interpret every shriek in the trees, is still doing its work, latching on to the slamming of doors and the flushing of toilets in unknown precincts of the building. The sky is a chemical orange colour.

Being unable to sleep night after night, for weeks on end, is – of course – hell. But in smaller doses, insomnia in a lonely foreign hotel does not need a cure. It's an asset with some key troubles of the soul. Crucial things you need to think about get a chance to unfold here. During the day, back home, you are dutiful to others, you're part of a team of 30. The emails come in by the dozen every ten minutes. Here, for once, in this box at the end of a long corridor, you can return to a bigger duty: to yourself.

The hotel on the edge of the runway is a corrective to the demands of the community, to the inability to think in the normal press of the day. It's like a monastery in the times of old. You can turn things over. The thoughts of this long night would sound weird to your partner, your friends, your children. These people need you to be a certain way. They cannot tolerate all your possibilities and desires – and for some good reasons. You don't want to let them down; they have a right to benefit from your predictability. But their expectations choke off important aspects of who you are.

Now, in this endless night by the airport, with the window open and a clearing sky above, it is just you, the universe and an A380 on its final approach from Dubai.

In the rush of the day, there is no time for the higher-order questions: where is my career going? How come there is so little tenderness in my relationship? How could I reconnect with my kids? What do I really want from this brief life? To be turning over such issues and yet to feel like a mere beginner is worrying, but you go with it nevertheless. You're taking notes on the hotel pad. You have the protection of the night and of a foreign land where no one knows of you or cares about you in the slightest. You could disappear here and hardly leave a trace.

You are naturally very inclined to want to be normal. Yet thanks to this insomnia, you are granted a crucial encounter with your weirder, truer self. The daytime-office you is a misleading picture of what you're like. This insomnia is a gift, and this lonely plastic hotel is its precious, unexpected, generous guardian.

8

Sunbathing

You haven't come to Rhodes to explore the medieval old town or the ancient temple of Apollo. You've not been drawn by a longing to try the local delicacy of chickpea fritters and unsalted ewe's milk cheese. Your more sophisticated acquaintances would think it trivial. But you have come here for just one thing: to get some sun.

On the beach, here, there are recliners under big straw sunshades. The water is warm. The heat envelops you and seems to ease the knotted muscles in your left shoulder.

Every day, the sky is perfectly blue and unclouded. From your hotel balcony, you look out onto an arid, scrubby hill; you love the sight of the baked and cracked earth because it speaks of week after week of hot, dry weather. For months – practically for your whole life, it feels – you have been craving sunshine.

In the north, the environment doesn't feel benign. It can't be trusted. You are always fending off something: the wind, the rain, the cold. Through the impossibly long winter and wintry spring, you have been swaddling yourself in layers of garments. You hardly ever see your own legs – beyond a reluctant glance at their pasty paleness in the bath. You seriously wonder if anyone could find your body attractive these days. You eat for comfort. You're always wanting scones or pies or big helpings of apple crumble. And it shows – somewhere under the habitual jumpers and coats.

But deep within you, you feel as if you are a creature essentially made for sunny mornings, hot, lazy afternoons and warm nights. That's where you, *Homo sapiens*, were designed to live. But by ingenious, effortful and it seems rather fateful manoeuvres, we humans have managed to sustain ourselves in fundamentally alien places that are reliably windswept, wet, icy and dreary for most of the year and only fitfully, capriciously anything else. We've made good lives for ourselves up there – in Wiesbaden, Trondheim, Hyvinkää and Calgary. But at a cost.

Sunshine isn't merely 'nice'. It has a profound role in our lives. It is an agent of moral qualities: of generosity, courage, the appreciation of the present moment, confidence ... When the world seems bountiful, material accumulation looks less impressive. When there is easy living, competition loses its edge. When it is so hot, there is no point trying to read – or even think too much. One is merely in the present.

These are corrective attitudes. Too much of them and they turn against themselves. If the ways of the north are too dominant and entrenched in your life, you need the virtues of the south. You have come to lie on the beach at Pefkos not because you are light-minded or indolent. But precisely because you have become – by habit – so dutiful, serious, hard-working, disconnected from your body, over-cerebral and cautious.

It is a deeply noble search for wisdom and balance (which are the ideal goals of art and civilisation) that has led you here – to the world of sun cream, dark glasses, recliners and vividly coloured cocktails by the pool.

The Desert

You are – quite literally – in the middle of nowhere and, unexpectedly, it's helping. A lot. How frantic we otherwise normally are. We live competitive crazed lives: we compare ourselves constantly to those who have more, are smarter, seem more organised, look younger …

There are so many reasons to be frantic, and yet – as we know in our hearts – it is even more of a priority to keep an occasional appointment with someone we neglect in our normal madness: a deeper, quieter part of ourselves. We have intimations of it at night, on the motorway or in the grey stillness of the early morning. And we feel it strongly here, deep in Navajo land, on the Utah–Arizona border.

It seems everything we do matters so much, but, here, we listen to a different, more humbling message: that everything we do and are is in truth meaningless – when considered from a sufficient distance, from the perspective of the timeless stones, the boundless vistas, the infinite heavens.

To counter our tendencies to exaggerate and panic, we need only meditate on our utter insignificance when measured against aeons of time and space. It was 200 million years ago that the Triassic seas retreated and the land rose up to become a high desert plateau that wind and rain have slowly, ever so slowly eroded. Harder capstones gradually emerged, protecting the rock below, to form the slender pinnacles, or buttes, and wider mesas of Monument Valley.

It is baking hot here during the day. The air is thin. It is a place resolutely indifferent to our lives. Here one does not matter; it is obvious – in a quiet, not-unkind way – that one's life is a tiny thing. The desert provides a needed, strategic renewal of perspective.

Beyond the dramatic pillars of rock, the empty, very slightly undulating table extends into infinity without any mark of mankind. A light haze builds at the horizon. Banks of distant cloud are touched with pink and gold as the sun starts to go down, the horizontal rays of the sun setting the upright bands of sandstone alight. The ego is loosened, forgets itself.

The desert rehearses in grand terms a lesson that ordinary life typically introduces viciously: that the universe is mightier than we are; that we are frail and temporary and have no alternative but to accept the limitations on our will; that we must bow to necessities greater than ourselves. This is the lesson written into the stones and the red sands. But so grandly is it written here that we can come away from the desert, not crushed, but inspired by what lies beyond us, privileged to be subject to such majestic necessities.

We have not only travelled to a place, we have heard the whispers, across an ochre wasteland, of a philosophy of wisdom.

10

Finding Your Feet Abroad

On the first day, it was difficult. You went into the corner shop just off the main Motomachi shopping street to buy a prepaid mobile card. You pointed at your phone; you pretended to make a call. It was useless. Mr Nishimura couldn't understand you at all. You were hot and flustered (it was 86 degrees Fahrenheit and pretty humid). You felt such an idiot.

It was eerily familiar: like the time at school you were supposed to make a speech and your mind went totally blank; the painful evenings at college when everybody else seemed to be heading off somewhere and you weren't sure if you could ask to join in.

Over the years, at home, you have learned how to avoid many of the situations that you find so awkward (though other people appear to manage them without the slightest concern). Most of the time, you can work round the diffidence and fear of being the unwelcome focus of attention, what at certain moments you call your shyness. When something feels alien or in any way threatening, your instinct is to retreat. You'd never ask a stranger for directions in the street; the idea of going up to a group of people you don't know at a party is terrifying. But now you are beginning to tire of the downside of this survival tactic: the too-high price it extracts.

In Japan, everything is, to you, foreign. You of course can't know what you are supposed to do. You are so far from being inconspicuous, it's a joke. Shyness is in a way no longer even an option. You are already so far off the deep end.

So you go back to the shop. You make use of the ATM (which has an English language option). You buy some wasabi-flavoured crisps and give the man a big smile. He grins back. You're learning to be a little more confident. You are learning how to do something: you're learning to overcome, not just work round, your shyness. A holiday that immerses you in a life entirely different to your normal routine is the ideal setting to exercise what is really a skill (though we tend to see it as a piece of good or bad luck). You didn't book into a big chain hotel. You've rented an apartment near the wonderful Sankeien Gardens from a really nice guy called Kazutaka.

Today you bought a packet of Chokobi mini star-shaped chocolate biscuits. You made a joke about the rain. You said 'ame desu' – which you'd practised after breakfast and hopefully means something like 'it's raining' – and gestured drolly at your wet hair. Mr Nishimura beamed at you. It's a deep corrective. The people in your life who have been hard to please do not represent normality.

A small pleasure – as little as smiling across a linguistic gulf – is often really a satisfaction in glimpsing a great and useful truth manifest in an eloquent detail. The movement of the facial muscles of the shopkeeper are a tiny, welcome, announcement of a profound fact: there is a vast quantity of goodwill circulating in the world just below the surface and which we usually delve into too rarely. But now perhaps we can more often. We can take this growth in confidence with us when we go back home. There is less to fear.

11

Being up Late at Night

It's very late; more conventional people have long ago turned in, but we have stayed up, to read, to think, to talk with a long-forgotten person: ourselves. Late at night is when big things may at last have a chance to happen in the mind.

Night is a corrective to the demands of the community. I may be a dentist or a maths teacher but, long before that happened and still now when I am allowed to commune with myself, I am simply a nameless, limitless consciousness, a far more expansive, un-anchored figure, of infinite possibilities and rare, disturbing, ambivalent, peculiar, visionary insights.

The thoughts of night would sound weird to my mother, my friend, my boss, my child. These people need us to be a certain way. They cannot tolerate all our possibilities and for some good reasons. We don't want to let them down; they have a right to benefit from our predictability. But their expectations shape us, make us who we are, and choke off important aspects.

However, at night, with the window open and a clear sky above, it is just us and the universe – and for a time, we can take on a little of its boundlessness.

12

The Charm of Cows

- It's weird they exist at all.
- You can't tell what a cow is thinking, though it's definitely thinking something.
- Cows look great in fields.
- They are easy-going: a clump of grass, a bale of hay make them happy; they don't mind standing in the drizzle.
- Cows are not selfish.
- If you look at a cow for five minutes, a tiny part of its tranquil soul takes root in you.
- Their ears were designed by a comic genius.
- Apart from that, they carefully protect their dignity.
- Cows are slightly bigger than you think.
- Cows have never rebelled. They harbour no bitterness. They are expert at waiting.
- A cow does not judge you: you are what you are, to a cow.
- Cows don't fidget.
- They appear to be shy.
- By chance, many people drink their breast milk.
- They have no faith in politics.
- Cows do not suffer from status anxiety.
- Cows are not interested in what you think of them.
- Cows do not dwell on their troubles.
- Nothing you do will ever amuse or impress a cow.
- Cows are very focused on now.
- Looking at cows can make your day.

13

Up at Dawn

It's 5.45 am on a summer's morning. You've woken early. It's still outside. The sun hasn't quite risen yet. Normally, you'd be sleeping right through this. You're reconnecting with your life. Somewhere, a solitary lorry rumbles away. The forecast says it's going to be hot later. All the real brightness and warmth is still beyond the horizon. But it's on its way. It's started to turn the lower clouds orange and make the sky, in that direction, pink and pale purple. The bottom clouds look like they are floating in a golden sea. If you haven't seen it for a while, you forget how impressive it looks. Every single morning some version of this happens, though you are almost always asleep when it does.

In the kitchen, there are a few last remains of yesterday. The argument you had last night feels far away. Why did it matter? Dawn is the world's reminder to let yesterday go. When everyone else is asleep, the house feels like it is just yours. You can remember why you like it.

Last night in here it was quite tense while you were cooking dinner. Your partner was giving you a hard time – at least you thought they were. No one else is going to be up for ages. You've got the place to yourself. It looks different at this hour. The magical square of early sunlight on the wall makes you think of childhood. You on Sunday mornings, when your parents had a lie-in; you'd sneak down and steal biscuits. It felt like going for an adventure – in your own home.

You can hear the birds, now. Later, the human world will drown them out. Overnight, a snail has made a momentous journey from the windowsill to a potted geranium. At dawn you notice things that are missed in the rush of the day. There are parts of yourself that get missed too. More delicate, more wondering. You've been missing the version of yourself that you only meet at this time.

You head out to pick up a few things from a local shop. The air feels blissfully fresh. And it's quiet. The usual roar of traffic from the main road hasn't started. There's a brief flap of wings as a bird rises from a nearby tree. You can hear a clear, high-pitched bird call and another very different one, more hollow and warm. The details of the natural world so easily escape our notice.

You see a tranquil beauty in the tower block you've always rather disliked up to now. You feel friendly towards a man with cropped grey hair who is noisily stacking shopping baskets and boxes of bananas outside the supermarket. There's someone walking their dog. Like you – at least today – a voluntary early riser; they've chosen to be here. You don't know anything else about them, except this one thing, which, at the moment, seems important. You almost say hello. Maybe another time you will. You stroll across the road – usually you have to wait for the lights and scurry over. You've got time to watch the clouds shed their pink tones and take on their normal smudged appearance. At this hour, it's a little easier to think well of the world. The city looks serene and elegant. You feel calm and a little proud of yourself for being here now.

You have a burst of energy for things you often don't want to face. You map out the pros and cons of a career move on a big sheet of paper; you look through some old family photographs and send a long email to your mother; you pay a couple of annoying bills online and get them out of the way; you cook yourself a good breakfast of scrambled eggs.

It's strange: all available time is, in truth, limited. You can't make there be 25 hours in the day. Yet now it does feel like you are in possession of an extra slice of existence; it's always been there, but you've only just found it. Time could be rearranged: there are plenty of things that can contribute to leading a life more like the one we want. We could get new chances. Every day, it happens. And every day you have the chance to be again the person you are just now in the very early morning.

Staring out of the Window

We tend to reproach ourselves for staring out of the window. We are supposed to be working, or studying, or ticking off things on our to-do list. It can seem almost the definition of wasted time. It seems to produce nothing, to serve no purpose. We equate it with boredom, distraction, futility. The act of cupping our chin in our hands near a pane of glass and letting our eyes drift in the middle distance does not normally enjoy high prestige. We don't go around saying: 'I had a great day: the high point was staring out of the window'. But maybe in a better society that's just the sort of thing people would say to one another.

The point of staring out of a window is, paradoxically, not to find out what is going on outside. It is, rather, an exercise in discovering the contents of our own minds. It's easy to imagine we know what we think, what we feel and what's going on in our heads. But we rarely do entirely. There's a huge amount of what makes us who we are that circulates unexplored and unused. Its potential lies untapped. It is shy and doesn't emerge under the pressure of direct questioning. If we do it right, staring out of the window offers a way for us to listen out for the quieter suggestions and perspectives of our deeper selves.

Plato suggested a metaphor for the mind: our ideas are like birds fluttering around in the aviary of our brains. But in order for the birds to settle, Plato understood that we needed periods of purpose-free calm. Staring out of the window offers such an opportunity. We see the world going on: a patch of weeds is holding its own against the wind; a grey tower block looms through the drizzle. But we don't need to respond; we have no overarching intentions, and so the more tentative parts of ourselves have a chance to be heard, like the sound of church bells in the city once the traffic has died down at night.

The potential of daydreaming isn't recognised by societies obsessed with productivity. But some of our greatest insights come when we stop trying to be purposeful and instead respect the creative potential of reverie. Window daydreaming is a little strategic rebellion against the excessive demands of immediate (but ultimately insignificant) pressures – in favour of the diffuse, but very serious, search for the wisdom of the unexplored deep self.

Some pleasures – like that of looking out of a window and wondering about life – are so quiet that we easily miss them. We don't quite detect them, even though they are really there – as one may fail to catch a whispered endearment in a noisy bar. But once properly alerted we can better direct our attention to something that turns out to be tender and lovely. Small pleasures are often of this kind. It is the task of culture to draw them to our notice, so that they can take up a larger, beneficial place in our lives.

A Hot Bath

It is easy to get carried away imagining a happy life. One mentally sketches the perfect job, the ideal relationship, a wide set of fascinating yet always cheerful friends.

It's lovely to think about such things, but to get very attached to these hopes is unhelpful: life perhaps just won't live up to them. One will be forever disappointed. Which is why there's a wisdom that focuses on the reliable pleasures and satisfaction that lie within our grasp. A hot bath fits into this category.

It's best when the water is deep and, at first, almost too hot. You venture a foot, wince, and run a burst of cold. Slowly you lower yourself in. The water surges up round your sides as you go down, a little wave goes over the side – but you'll live with that. You lie back and put a foot up by the taps, getting one knee into the warmth. Then you change legs.

There's a little surge of gratitude as you think for what a tiny sliver of history this easy comfort has been around. This apparently modest achievement (a tub of liquid heated to X per cent of body temperature) is the outcome of epic labours: dams and reservoirs were constructed on distant rivers; people with broken fingernails laid the pipes; long-dead inventors fretted at night to come up with the prototype non-drip tap; wind farm entrepreneurs, nuclear scientists, frogmen on oil rigs and mining engineers have ensured that hot water is constantly on hand.

The bath allows us to be both uncovered and cosy. Unless we inhabit a few favoured zones of the globe, the physical environment is normally dispiritingly hostile: by day we have to swaddle our skin in careful layers of wool and cotton and, at night, encase ourselves within sheets and duvets. Then, briefly, in the bath, none of that is necessary. A bath is an artificially warm afternoon in midsummer. It is a return to the easy nakedness of our primal ancestors. And it echoes too the months when we first floated in warm water, in the little sealed bath of the womb, soothed by the rumblings of our mother's digestive tract and growing a pancreas and some toes to the rhythm of her heart. The bath hints to the body of its distant past of complete contentment, before it was propelled across the horizon of birth into the imperfect world.

But the pleasure of the bath is primarily intellectual. Baths are ideal places to think. Their ability to ease us towards productive ideas is probably greater than that of the places we formally assign to such work: the office, the seminar room, the library or the laboratory. The reason is that our bigger thoughts generally don't come when commanded. They tend to emerge when we're not quite looking, like shy deer reluctant to come out of the shadows of the forest for fear of the hunter. The warm water lulls the nervous habits of the mind. We're off the hook. We're perfectly free not to think at all and – by the perverse logic of the brain – this actually makes thinking easier. We can risk being totally wrong, we can imagine adventurous scenarios, and our fixed ideas can be set aside just long enough for novel, and potentially better, ones to get a hearing.

Religions have long been ambitious around bathing. Hindu priests taught their followers to immerse themselves in the waters of the Ganges. In the ceremony to mark conversion to Judaism, the candidate enters a deep pool.

Christian baptism originally involved complete submersion. Religions sent people into water at big moments: when turning over a new leaf, starting afresh, getting another chance. As quite often happens in secular life, we are tentatively recreating for ourselves personal versions of ancient sacred rituals. It's not actually surprising that this happens, because religions were deeply concerned with the way a physical act – such as bathing – can affect the mind. They were very interested in getting devotees into the right mental state and were keen to use any resource that could help. Over a very long time they accumulated great expertise. We may not share their ultimate framework of belief, but their insight into the way in which the body can be the means of influencing the psyche are still useful. We too can turn to the bath when we wish to get ourselves into a better mental state.

At a distance, we're following in the footsteps of the great religions when we shut the bathroom door and turn on the hot tap. We're not just looking to get clean. We're trying to move on from the painful, offensive aspects of the day. We're hoping the trauma will dissolve and gently loosen itself from us in the water. We're seeking to liberate the better ambitions of our minds via a comfortable soak in the steaming waters of the bath.

16

Indulgent Pessimism

We'd not normally think that pessimism – anticipating the worst and taking the darker view of existence – could be a source of pleasure. But behind its dour reputation, it harbours elements of a kind and generous philosophy. Which makes sense when we consider the origins of this way of thinking. Pessimism was developed mainly in ancient Rome and principally by the dramatist and political adviser Seneca and, later, the Emperor Marcus Aurelius. They weren't killjoys. Pessimism was a calculated strategy to safeguard happiness in a troubled and dangerous world. They were fascinated by the corrosive power of disappointment. Inflated expectations and hopes can rob anyone – no matter how good things objectively are – of satisfaction. We get miserable not because things are necessarily really so awful, but because they fall short of the standard we have demanded. To anticipate the worst is, curiously, a cheering attitude. Life isn't incidentally miserable, pessimism tells us: it is fundamentally deeply difficult for everyone.

Here are a few of the small pleasures of pessimistic thoughts:

We reassure ourselves about the amount of time we have left by pegging our imagined death to the date of the average lifespan, without remembering that long before we reach that terminal point we will have passed through years of growing infirmity, terror as our friends die off, a sense that we no longer feel at home in the world, a humiliation that anyone doing anything significant is decades younger than us, embarrassing bladder problems and our own sexual repulsiveness. In other words: we must never hold back from a useful panic at how little time there is left.

When we resolve one major anxiety, we imagine that we will be satisfied and calm will descend. But all we're really ever doing is freeing up space for an even more poisonous and aggressive worry to spring forth, as it always will. Life can only ever be a process of replacing one anxiety with another.

The greatest part of our suffering is brought about by our hopes (for health, happiness and success). Therefore, the kindest thing we can do for ourselves is to recognise that our griefs are not incidental or passing, but a fundamental aspect of existence which will only get worse – until the worst of all happens.

The only people we can think of as normal are those we don't yet know very well.

We reserve a special place in our hearts for those who can't see the point of us. Instead of ignoring them, we will take their scepticism deep into our hearts and spend much of our lives inventing strategies to persuade them of our worth – and we will never succeed.

The best way to be a calmer and nicer person is to give up on everyone. No one will appreciate you as you deserve; you will never fully satisfy the needs of another. The route to tolerance and patient good humour is to realise that one simply is, where it counts, irredeemably alone.

True wisdom is the recognition of just how often wisdom will simply not be an option. In theory, we'd love to meet trouble calmly, be poised in the face of opposition, react with humility to criticism and peacefully accept the fact that we will be outdistanced by people we don't like. But the fact is we'll squirm and get upset and panic and descend into rage. We'll never be fully mature. We'll always rebel against certain painful truths. And it's wise to admit this about ourselves.

Worldly success is the consolation prize for those unhappy driven souls who have redirected their early humiliation and sense that they weren't good enough into 'achievements' – which will never make up for the unconditional love they will deep down always crave in vain.

Rather than imagining that they might feel guilt, people who have hurt us, in fact, typically start to hate us – for reminding them of their own meanness.

For paranoia about 'what other people think', remember that very few love, only some hate – and nearly everyone just doesn't care.

We have begun to know someone properly whenever they have started substantially to disappoint us.

Choosing a person to marry is just a matter of deciding what particular kind of suffering we would like to commit ourselves to.

The cure for infatuation is to get to know the object of one's desire better. Soon their inevitable defects will be revealed.

The pleasure of pessimism isn't linked to being mean or bitter. It's grounded, in fact, on sympathy. This is an antidote to the oppressive modern demand to look only on the bright side. It allows us to bond with others around an honest admission of some truly sobering realities.

17

Self-Pity

We learned self-pity when we were young. It was a sunny Sunday afternoon; you were 9 years old. Your parents wouldn't let you have any ice cream if you didn't do your maths homework. It was achingly unfair. Every other child in the world was playing football or watching television. No one else has such a mean mother. It was just awful.

We're all – in theory – dead against self-pity. It seems deeply unattractive because it reveals egoism in its most basic form: the failure to put our own suffering into proper perspective against the larger backdrop of human history. We lament our tiny disasters and look coldly on the grand tragedies of the world. A problem with one's fringe or a wrongly cooked steak dominates the mind while we ignore work conditions in China and the Gini coefficient of Brazil.

No one likes to own up to self-pity. And yet, if we are honest, it's something we feel quite often. And in fact it's often a rather sweet emotion.

The fact is, we do deserve a great deal more pity than other people are ever very likely to bestow upon us. Life is, in truth, horrendously hard in many ways – even if one does have a top-notch data plan and an elegantly designed fridge. Our talents are never fairly recognised, our best years will necessarily drift away, and we won't find all the love we need. We deserve pity and there isn't anyone else around to give it to us, so we have to supply a fair dose of it to ourselves. The operative cause might from a lofty perspective seem ridiculous – poor me, I'll never drive a Ferrari; it's so sad, I thought we were going to a Japanese restaurant and they've booked a pub. But these are just the convenient opportunities for immersing ourselves in a much bigger issue: the fundamental sorrows of existence, for which we do – genuinely – deserve the most tender compassion.

Imagine what things would be like if we couldn't pity ourselves. We would be that far worse category of mental discomfort: depressed. The depressed person is someone who has lost the art of self-pity, who has become too rigorous with themselves. If you think of a parent comforting a child, they often spend hours on a very minor thing: a lost toy, nonou's broken eye, the children's party to which one was not invited. They are not being ridiculous; they are in effect teaching the child how to look after themselves – and giving space to the important idea that 'small' upsets can have very large internal consequences. Gradually we learn to mimic this parental attitude with ourselves and come to be able to feel sorry for ourselves when no one else will. It's not necessarily entirely rational, but it's a coping mechanism. A first protective shell which we develop in order to be able to manage some of the immense disappointments and frustrations that life throws at us. The defensive posture of self-pity is far from contemptible. It is touching and important. Many religions have given expression to this attitude by inventing deities who look with inexpressible pity upon human beings. In Catholicism, for instance, the Virgin Mary is often presented as weeping out of tenderness for the miseries of the normal human life. Such kindly beings are really projections of our own need to be pitied.

Self-pity is compassion we extend to ourselves. A more mature aspect of the self turns to the weak and lost parts of the psyche and comforts them, strokes them, tells them it understands and that they are indeed lovely but misunderstood. It allows them to be, for a while, a bit babyish – since that is actually what they are. It provides the undemanding, confirming love every baby, but far more importantly, every adult, needs to get through the anguish of existence.

Crushes

You are introduced to someone at a conference. They look nice and you have a brief chat about the theme of the keynote speaker. But already, partly because of the slope of their neck and a lilt in their accent, you have reached an overwhelming conclusion. Or, you sit down in the carriage and there, diagonally opposite you, is someone you cannot stop looking at for the rest of a journey across miles of darkening countryside. You know nothing concrete about them. You are going only by what their appearance suggests. You note that they have slipped a finger into a book (*The Food of the Middle East*), that their nails are bitten raw, that they have a thin leather strap around their left wrist and that they are squinting a touch short-sightedly at the map above the door. And that is enough to convince you. Another day, coming out of the supermarket, amidst a throng of people, you catch sight of a face for no longer than eight seconds and yet, here too, you feel the same overwhelming certainty – and, subsequently, a bittersweet sadness at their disappearance in the anonymous crowd.

Crushes happen to some people often and to almost everyone sometimes. Airports, trains, streets, conferences – the dynamics of modern life are forever throwing us into fleeting contact with strangers, from amongst whom we pick out a few examples who seem to us not merely interesting, but, more powerfully, the solution to our lives. This phenomenon – the crush – goes to the heart of the modern understanding of love. It could seem like a small incident, essentially comic and occasionally farcical. It may look like a minor planet in the constellation of love, but it is in fact the underlying secret central sun around which our notions of the Romantic revolve.

A crush represents in pure and perfect form the dynamics of Romantic philosophy: the explosive interaction of limited knowledge, outward obstacles to further discovery – and boundless hope.

The crush reveals how willing we are to allow details to suggest a whole. We allow the arch of someone's eyebrow to suggest a personality. We take the way a person puts more weight on their right leg as they stand listening to a colleague as an indication of a witty independence of mind. Or their way of lowering their head seems proof of a complex shyness and sensitivity. From only a few cues, you anticipate years of happiness, buoyed by profound mutual sympathy. They will fully grasp that you love your mother even though you don't get on well with her; that you are hard-working, even though you appear to be distracted; that you are hurt rather than angry. The parts of your character that confuse and puzzle others will at last find a soothing, wise, complex soulmate.

The truth is, though, that the person around whom we are building these thoughts will in reality inevitably be quite different from the way we picture them. They will indeed have many lovely qualities. But they will also have problems, failings, weaknesses and frankly annoying characteristics. They will have been scarred in some way or another by childhood, they will have pockets of deep selfishness, there will be things that really matter to us that they will find incomprehensible or offensive. If we tried to put a crush into practice and settled down with this individual (as our fantasy prompts) we'd find all this out soon enough.

In order to enjoy a crush we have to understand that that is what it is. If we think that we are in fact encountering a person who will make us happy, who will actually be the ideal person to live and grow old with, we are – inadvertently – destroying the specific satisfaction the crush brings. The pleasure depends on our recognising that we are imagining an ideal person, not really finding one.

To crush well is to realise that the lovely person we sketch in our heads is our creation: a creation that says more about us than about them. But what it says about us is important. The crush gives us access to our own ideals. We may not really be getting to know another person properly, but we are growing our insight into who we really are.

Keeping Your Clothes On

There's an assumption at large that sexiness is at heart about nakedness and explicitness: and that logically, therefore, the sexiest scenarios must also be the ones involving the greatest amounts of nudity.

But the truth about excitement is likely to be rather different. At the core of sexiness is an idea: the idea of being allowed into someone's life, when the memory of having been excluded from it is at its most vivid. Sexiness stems from the contrast between prohibition and acceptance. It is a species of relief and thanks at being given permission to touch and go anywhere.

Oddly, this gratitude is likely to be most prevalent not when one has been granted full licence by someone – but when one is on the borderline, when one has only just been lent a pass, and when the memory of the taboo of sex which surrounds most people is still intense. The reminder of the danger of rejection brings the wonder at being included into sharp, ecstatic relief.

This explains why the decision to keep one's clothes on a bit longer than strictly necessary, to deliberately keep clothes on during sex, can prove such a turn-on. To heighten excitement, we may design a scenario in which we are 'allowed' only to press against one another, never moving beyond guilty caresses and small thrusts – like we might have been forced to do in early adolescence or Saudi Arabia.

By staying clothed, we're retaining the erotic power of anticipation. There's a particular thrill in the early stages of an encounter – when you're almost inadvertently, it might seem, extending your arm along the back of a sofa and lightly brushing your fingers against the top of their jumper, a few inches below the nape of their lovely neck; or tentatively exploring a booted leg under a restaurant table (while maintaining an engaging flow of conversation about French gardens or the future of the Eurozone); or when someone bends down to rescue a peanut from the carpet, making a calculated display just for you, their T-shirt stretching over a muscular shoulder, or a delicate collarbone framed by a little black dress.

Such games mean we can keep revisiting the incredible idea of permission: the outer garments evoke the barriers one has finally been able to cross with impunity. Playfully limiting oneself to pressing through wool and cotton brings into enticing alignment both one's previous exclusion and the new wondrous inclusion.

The rule that we know full well is fake – ('don't go very far') – makes our status as actual lovers all the more vivid and hence arousing. We are, via the game, trying to get over a trauma around exclusion.

Rather than the prohibition being out of our hands (as it usually is with people we desire), here – with our accepting partner – it can by contrast be willed: one is in control of what was previously painfully out of one's grasp. Prudishness is invited into the game as a way of exorcising the difficulties it once caused us. Now, appropriated into sex, it is stripped of its sting and used to reaffirm a fresh confidence about being acceptable.

Once we are used to being undressed around someone, the wonder that they've allowed us into their lives is liable to get lost and taken for granted. We might end up watching television naked after a shower, with no one caring to note how special our unclothed selves still really are. The game of keeping one's clothes on tries to keep the interest of nakedness alive for a little longer by drawing attention to the privileges of permission. The game symbolises a poignant desire fully to savour the beauty of being, at last, allowed...

20

Kissing

Of course, we know already how nice kissing is. The point of dwelling on it isn't to guide attention freshly to something we'd hardly realised could be so nice. Rather, it's to renew and deepen our appreciation of a familiar enjoyment.

Mutual desire is normally signalled by a pretty weird act: two organs otherwise used for eating and speaking are rubbed and pressed against one another with increasing force, accompanied by the secretion of saliva. A tongue normally precisely manipulated to articulate vowel sounds, or to push mashed potato or broccoli to the rear of the palate, now moves forward to meet its counterpart, whose tip it might touch in repeated staccato movements. One would have to carefully explain to an alien visitor from Kepler-9b what is going on. These people, one would reassure the interstellar visitor, are not about to bite chunks out of each other's cheeks; they are not attempting to inflate one another ('please try to forget for a moment everything we were saying earlier about party balloons; there's no connection').

Reminding ourselves of the inherently bizarre nature of the act helps us to be usefully puzzled by, and newly curious about, why kissing is so significant and potentially so exciting. If it's so strange, why do we really love doing it?

Sexual excitement is psychological. It's not so much what our bodies happen to be doing that is getting us so turned on. It's what's happening in our brains that matters.

Partly, the excitement of kissing is the result of social codes. It's not purely natural or intrinsic that pinioning your lips to those of another person is so significant. We could imagine a society where it was very important for two people to rub the gap between the index finger and thumb together. You'd thrust forward and get very turned on by the mutual friction of the abductor pollicis transversus muscles. You'd lie awake at night dreaming of doing this to someone but really unsure about how they would react. The first time you did it would be something you'd remember all your life. The huge meaning of kissing is something we've built up by social agreement, and its fundamental definition is: I accept you – accept you so much that I will take a big risk with you. It is on this basis that kissing isn't merely physically nice, but psychologically delightful.

Kissing is exciting because it could so easily be revolting. The inside of a mouth is deeply private. No one usually goes there outside of the dentist. It's yours alone. The thought of the mouth of someone you don't like is extremely creepy. Ordinarily it would be utterly nauseating to have a stranger poke their tongue into your face; the idea of their saliva lubricating your lips is horrendous. So to allow someone to do these things signals a huge level of acceptance. There's a special joy of touching someone's back teeth with your tongue which has nothing to do with the appeal of licking enamel. All of us suffer from strong feelings of unacceptability and shame, which another's kiss starts to work on overcoming.

Apart from the publicly overt person, everyone has a more elusive, deeper self, which is kept in reserve as far as other people are concerned and yet is hugely familiar from the inside. This deeper, private self is active in a serious kiss, which is what you feel you are getting and giving access to. In the kiss, our mouth becomes a privileged place in which we surrender our defences and gift ourselves to another. We are properly exposed and raw. Kissing is a pleasure, ultimately, because it signals something more exciting even than sex: a brief respite from loneliness.

There's a tradition of thought – which can be usefully labelled Romanticism – which is averse to analysing pleasures. It fears that to analyse a joy is to kill it. It's the fear that knowledge punctures the mystery on which the happy experience depends – as a conjuring trick loses its charm when the secret of how it is done is revealed. We are impressed by another, contrary, more Classical attitude that regards insight as a route to enhancing the sweetness of the moment. A small pleasure, such as kissing, frequently turns out to be connected to meeting a large need. The satisfaction we feel is our recognition of getting something that is truly important to us, even if we don't usually have a very explicit sense of what this is. So, investigating a pleasure – teasing out its meaning – yields a greater sense of appreciation. The pleasure becomes keener and more significant when we grasp why we feel it.

21

Children's Drawings

Today we tend to take it for granted that a child's drawing or painting can be very charming indeed. But unless we happen to be the parents of a 6-year-old or a fond grandparent, we probably don't think much about it. As frequently happens, we don't deny that such things can be very pleasing, it's just that we don't make a deliberate place for them in our lives – we leave it to chance. And years might go by in which the particular small pleasure of looking at a child's drawing is missing from one's existence.

Historically speaking, it's actually very odd that we have this pleasure at all. Until comparatively recently it was unthinkable that someone could lay claim to maturity, sanity and reliability by pinning a picture by a 6-year-old to the walls of their office, or throne room – or that any adult could be charmed by an image of someone with a wonky grin, their arms emerging horizontally from mid-torso, with three stubby fingers to each hand and with, apparently, no feet. Until late into the twentieth century, few people were ready to admire any kind of art that lacked a conspicuous command of technical skills and was sensitively faithful to the real appearance of things. The works of children seemed merely the clumsy efforts of complete beginners.

We've become much more willing to be pleased. But what is it about the artworks of the under-sevens that we now see special merit in? What needs in ourselves do we now begin to recognise that explains the delight we feel? (Pleasure, often, can be understood as the satisfaction of a need.) If we say that a child's drawing is sweet – what are we really getting at with that word 'sweet' and why do we seem to need this quality of sweetness so much at this point in history?

What often touches us in the art of children is a host of qualities that are deeply under threat in adult lives and yet which we unconsciously recognise as precious to a sense of inner balance and psychological well-being. The sweet is a vital part of ourselves – currently in exile.

One of the most recurring features of children's art is evidence of trust. So long as things have gone reasonably well, children can believe in surfaces: if mummy smiles, she must be OK. There is, at a young age, blessedly little room for ambiguity. Children are not always trying to peer below the surface and discover the compromises and evasions that belong to maturity. Their art functions as a highly necessary corrective to cynicism.

Adult lives seldom allow us not to be wary and suspicious. We grow to expect trouble to come from any direction. We are aware of the fragility of things, and how easily safety and hope can be crushed. It is rare to have 15 minutes without being submerged by a new wave of anxiety. It is therefore understandable if we turn with relief to the trusting attitude of those great diminutive artists, as brilliant at lifting our spirits as they are hopeless at delivering correct representations of an oak tree or a human face.

Another endearing and psychologically necessary quality of children's art is quite how inaccurate it tends to be. A traditional assumption of drawing is that being 'good' at it requires one to lay aside the demands of one's own ego in order to pay precise attention to what is actually out there. The artist must learn how to observe the world, and in order to do so must put a lot of themselves to one side.

Rather than being in any way painstaking or faithful, the child is gleefully unconcerned as to the true facts of the world. What is sweet is this daring lack of interest in 'getting it right' which symbolises a delightful freedom from concern about whether others will think it right or not either. Again, the term sweetness is our way of acknowledging that this is something we need to do a little more of in our own lives but find very hard to ask for directly. It's totally understandable that we learn, as adults, to accommodate ourselves to the needs of reality and of other people. But we can devote ourselves to this goal with so much zeal that our souls dry up.

It is not, in fact, strange that it is this period of human history that has been the first to get really interested in the sweetness of children. Societies get sensitive to things that they are missing. We live in a world of highly complex technology, extreme precision in science, massive bureaucracies, insecurity and intense meritocratic competition. To survive with any degree of success in these conditions, we have to be exceptionally controlled, forward-thinking, reasonable and cautious creatures. However, we tend not to identify what has grown in short supply in our lives head on. It would be rare to say: we need more flights of fancy, more innocent trust, more gleeful disregard of expectations ... We have forgotten that this is what we even want. Instead, we simply find it moving – in fact, sweet – to encounter these things in symbolic forms in the scribblings of a child.

Children's art provides an opportunity to start to get to know our own needs. They are, in their own way, political demands, compact manifestos for some of the things we urgently need a little more of in the anxious, compromised conditions of contemporary adult life.

Crimes in the Newspaper

You've had an argument with the children. Later you'll have to go to work and bite your tongue around your boss. Now you're in the bath, reading the newspaper. There's a big story on the front page. A Californian chef, on becoming convinced that his wife was having an affair, dismembered her and boiled her body parts for four days. Only a few bits of her skull were left – it was from these fragments that she was identified. Then you read that a couple living near Luton, claiming to offer financial advice, befriended and then poisoned a sequence of elderly clients. Another story informs you about a woman in Spain who stabbed her neighbour 13 times: for months the woman's dog had been barking during the day while she was at work (she was a dental hygienist); the neighbour complained repeatedly, left threatening notes, had called the police on multiple occasions and once kicked the dog in the street. Then the dog disappeared and was never found. Two days later the neighbour's body was discovered. Or you get intrigued by the story of a mid-ranking administrator in the Australian health service who turns out to have forged numerous contracts for the supply of medical equipment and to have spent the money on luxury shopping – in the last two years before he was caught, his purchases included 47 Louis Vuitton suitcases and 11 Patek Philippe watches.

From a distance, it hardly makes sense at all that we should find these things a source of pleasure. The stories deal with obviously horrible, horrendous things. But, strangely, it is reassuring, and even (though we don't relish saying so) enjoyable to hear about them. We perhaps worry that by taking pleasure in reading of them we are endorsing the crimes themselves. But the truth is we're not actively egging on criminals, we're not glad these things happened. On the contrary, it's the very fact that they are clearly so wrong that generates our moments of satisfaction.

One source of our pleasure is that in many ways these people look so normal. The chef reminds you of a cheeky boy in the classroom when you were a kid. The woman with the dog is like someone you just saw at the supermarket. We mostly encounter the edited versions of other people, while we are continually exposed to the unedited version of ourselves. The unfair comparison means we inevitably feel much weirder than we really are. There's that strange sexual thing that excites you. You feel like crying when you get stuck in traffic. In groups, you have the strange sense that everyone is normal except you. At work, you feel the need to laugh at a remark which, in all honesty, strikes you as entirely unamusing.

This is where the newspaper criminals come in. They have redrawn the scale of strangeness. By being exposed as 50 times more strange, they reposition our own lonely peculiarities squarely back in the realm of the humdrum and average. It has absolutely never even crossed your mind to cook your partner. You have lived a life free of the desire to collect designer luggage via defrauding hospitals; in the realm of poisoning and stabbing your neighbours, you are a snow-white innocent.

This is surely one of the hidden reasons middle-aged men turn in such numbers to reading books about Adolf Hitler. His catastrophic levels of insane rage, delusion, destructiveness and cruelty make pretty much everyone else look lovely by comparison. One may have spent the evening drinking beer, made three vaguely insulting remarks and omitted to brush one's teeth before coming to bed. But by the standards of Berchtesgaden, you are revealed as really rather nice.

It's not like you haven't had your share of challenges. You too have been deeply hurt by betrayal; you have wished for easy money and luxury possessions; you've had sour disputes with neighbours. But by comparison you have reacted with grace. You've felt furious, suffered from envy and had periods of money worries – but you never did what they did. You absorbed your pain rather than committed crimes. Their villainy reveals your quiet moral heroism.

23

Driving on the Motorway at Night

It's 10.15 pm. Usually, you'd be watching television, pottering in the kitchen in your socks, nibbling a biscuit, thinking about heading to bed. But instead you are behind the wheel, looking at the tail lights of cars comfortably far ahead, and with the occasional headlights slipping by on the other side; 117 miles to go at the last sign. We feel powerful and purposive. With only a tiny push the car surges forward along the wide, smooth lanes, past an HGV, round an expansive, lightly rising curve and into a long, even stretch under the comfortable pale glow of the road lighting. A blue sign invites others home to Nuneaton, and you feel a ripple of friendly goodwill to a place you've never visited and perhaps never will.

It's cosy in the car. Your craft is vigilantly monitoring its own well-being: the small lights on the display quietly indicate that all is well with the brake fluid, that the engine is happy with its temperature and that you are currently proceeding at 72 miles an hour. You are pleasantly contained, returned to a mobile womb able to roam safely across the darkened surface of the late-night world.

The pleasure one feels, though, isn't just to do with the cocooning environment. You are registering another kind of satisfaction as well – connected to what's going on inside your head. You are experiencing an underappreciated but important satisfaction that deserves a special name: driving therapy.

It's a strange, disturbing fact that the mind hates thinking. It's not something we much like admitting. But we're always dodging, jumping around, putting off turning a suspicion into a developed case; we withdraw from tricky mental confrontations with the failings of our preferred ideas and with troubling evidence. The monks of Buddhism took this difficulty very seriously – and they devised special environments to help themselves overcome these failings. They built remote monasteries and constructed gardens of moss and raked gravel; they investigated whether special ways of sitting would make a difference.

But they didn't have cars. Culturally, it's a long time since we've addressed the ideal preconditions for thinking. We deserve to integrate the car as a place for thought. And it's this pleasure – a pleasure of the mind – that we're registering as we cruise past the elegant curving exit ramp.

For thinking, surprisingly, complete stillness is not always the best environment for coaxing the mind towards its best efforts. Often a more helpful set-up is quiet plus motion plus something else not too taxing to be done. Driving provides multiple minor routines: checking the rear mirror, micro adjustments on the accelerator, the automatic scanning of the speedometer and the constant interplay of the hands on the wheel and the road ahead. In these circumstances, provided by the car, the nervous, censorious part of the mind is shut off. We're not so worried in advance about where a line of thought might go. We let the mind drift, helped along by the rhythmical passing of the overhead lamps. It can sound unproductive, but there's a hidden benefit when the mind wanders around a topic. We get out of mental ruts that are so familiar we don't even realise they are there. A possibility that gets closed off gets an airing – suppose one has been wrong? What if there's another strategy? What, in fact, is the big goal one is aiming at? Is there one? Perhaps one has been too critical, or too passive? New ways of seeing things come into view. And they do precisely because we're not trying too hard. We're entering the strange and highly useful territory in which we can entertain a thought without rushing quickly to endorse or condemn it – where we can wonder if something might be the case, without reaching too fast to decide. The car at night creates a benign mental climate in which some important thoughts get the chance to grow.

It's strangely attractive, at night in the middle of a long solo drive, to stop at a service station. Ordinarily that's got close to zero appeal. But now it's pleasing to change tempo, to sit silently amongst other human beings and have a coffee. Everyone is really a pilgrim, however well disguised they may seem to be. We are still far from home, but it's a helpful distance – from which we can for a while view more clearly the bigger outlines of existence.

Sunday Mornings

On weekdays you'd be out of the house by now, but to-day you're still in bed. You've got time to notice how the light is filtering through a gap in the curtains. It's quieter than usual outside; the background sound of traffic is muted. Down the road you hear a car door slam. There's not much you actually have to do today. You can dawdle in the bathroom. Normally you check your phone while brushing your teeth, rapidly scanning the messages that have come in overnight, mentally racing to keep track of all the things you'll have to be on top of for the day, as you struggle quickly into your work clothes. This morning it doesn't matter. You're briefly liberated from the pressure of watching the clock; you don't need to keep up. No one will be expecting anything of you until tomorrow morning. Out of the window the bands of clouds are drifting very, very slowly. It might rain this afternoon. There's the jacket you bought in Edinburgh; you haven't worn that for a while. You might head off to a café in a bit, maybe take a book or your journal, eat scrambled eggs with spinach; it could be nice to take a walk in the park later and see how the ducks are doing.

Sunday is a name for the time in which we can explore ourselves and discover, or rediscover, parts of ourselves that we haven't properly come to know as yet. Attention to them has been edged out in the most understandable ways by the demands of work and the expectations of others.

For a very long time, especially in the western world, the idea of Sunday was bound up with religion. It was the

Christian adaptation of the Jewish Sabbath: a day taken to have been set aside by God. The genius of the traditional religious concept of Sunday was to combine a set of restrictions with a positive agenda for the day. To ensure a day of rest there were various prohibitions. Businesses would be closed; shops, theatres and bars would be shut; the train timetable would be curtailed. The point wasn't to be joyless, it was to make sure that time was free for other things. Such collective rules have largely disappeared. But the underlying need remains: the time needs to be protected. One might decide to take a break from digital life, not read a newspaper, not to fill the day with routine administrative tasks. There's a real danger of filling up the day with distractions.

The other side of the traditional Sabbath was a contrastive set of expectations around the things you positively engaged with in this specially designated period of 24 hours – motivated by the thought that a day is long, but not infinite. It mustn't be squandered. One was supposed to go to church. Ceremonies were evolved to turn people's minds to questions that matter but that typically get marginalised: what am I doing with my life; how are my relationships going; what do I really value and why? The traditional idea of Sunday was framed in religious terms. But the needs that it addresses are actually entirely independent of that framework.

The secular pleasure of Sunday morning isn't simply one of relaxation and freedom; it's also linked to a feeling (which might not always be very explicit) that one has the opportunity to re-engage with the wider horizons of one's life.

The hope is that we can for a while turn away from current affairs towards the elevated, the silent and the eternal. We're reaching towards higher consciousness – though maybe not used to putting it in quite these terms. Normally, we're immersed in practical, unintrospective, self-justifying outlooks that are the hallmarks of what we could call 'lower' consciousness. At such moments, the world reveals itself as quite different: a place of suffering and misguided effort, full of people striving to be heard and lashing out against others, but also a place of tenderness and longing, beauty and touching vulnerability. The fitting response is universal sympathy and kindness. One's own life feels less precious; one can contemplate being no longer present with tranquillity. One's interests are put aside and one may imaginatively fuse with transient or natural things: trees, the wind, a moth, clouds or waves breaking on the shore. From this point of view, status is nothing, possessions don't matter, grievances lose their urgency. If certain people could encounter us at this point, they might be amazed at our transformation and at our new-found generosity and empathy.

States of higher consciousness are, of course, desperately short-lived. We shouldn't in any case aspire to make them permanent, because they don't sit so well with the many important practical tasks we all need to attend to. But we should make the most of them when they arise, and harvest their insights for the time when we require them most. A crucial part of the pleasure of Sunday morning is our awareness that it's a distinct, unusual time.

25

A Beloved's Wrist

You don't give it a second thought most of the time, of course. But in favoured circumstances – when it is framed by a leather watch strap, a crisp shirt cuff, a circle of amber stones or placed on a table, palm up – you notice again the especially delicate skin on the inside of the forearm, the interplay of gentle curves, swelling, flaring, narrowing, turning back in. The demands and complications of a relationship inevitably mean that you often don't feel particularly sweet and generous around this person – with whom you in fact spend so much of your existence. Just looking at this person's wrist can renew certain tender feelings that, you realise, you've been losing sight of.

Certain reasons why you love them can be rediscovered via contemplation of this strange hinge between the radial and carpal bones. The pleasure of looking at it is connected to remembering its history: how tiny it must have been when they were a baby, how it was once encased in woollen mittens, how they used to pull the cuff of a blue jumper down with their thumb (eventually wearing a little hole).

You are reconnecting with the grace of gestures they occasionally make and which deeply moved you when you were first infatuated with them, and which still have the power to touch you. There's a way they have of holding their hand up when pausing while typing at the keyboard while peering at the screen and biting their lower lip. It's a gesture of the wrist that indicates hesitancy, an anxious desire to get things right. Maybe it started when they had piano lessons aged 8½ and tried so hard to please

105

their teacher and play all the notes correctly. The desire to please is a side of them that you don't always see in daily life (especially when they are upbraiding you for not having quite accomplished your share of domestic responsibility).

You are drawn to the way they hold a knife when slicing a tomato – with the forefinger extended far out along the top of the blade and the wrist itself pushed down towards the chopping board: it's a strange action that only they seem to make. Watching them, you can trace a lifeline back to a more clumsy era of childhood, when it took great effort to control the blade; you are united across time with their earlier self, eager to learn, unclouded by the later complexities of existence. They can be pretty tough to be around sometimes, but the wrist is an emblem of the more fragile side of who they are.

They might be the only person in the world you could recognise by their wrist alone.

—

26

A Favourite Old Jumper

It's not one you can now really wear except at home – and maybe even only when you are on your own or have a good excuse: it's suddenly very cold; you're a bit poorly; you've just come back from a long trek in the country, it was raining, you have a shower and now you can get wonderfully cosy.

It used to be pretty smart, elastically moulding itself to your torso, close fitting at the wrists. Now it's expanded in weird ways, sagged, and the cuffs curl outwards; there's a hole in the left armpit.

When it was new, you wore it on a lovely afternoon in Copenhagen; it was with you the night you learned that X had had an affair; it came with you when you changed cities; once you slipped it on over your bare skin after you went skinny-dipping; it propped up your neck on a flight to Singapore; it helped you revise for an exam; once a lover bound your wrists with the sleeves. All these things live on in the jumper. When you bury your nose in it and breathe in, it takes you back to those times. It's lovely to wear it, curled up on the sofa, watching television. Only the people you truly love now ever get to see you in it.

With the jumper we rehearse something key. It is a transitional object that helps us along the path not from childhood to adulthood but towards old age.

The jumper works in opposition to a tendency – otherwise quite evident in lives – to fall out of love with things as they lose their original merits. It reverses the cold trajectory of growing disappointment: instead, love quietly accumulates round it. Without quite stating it plainly to ourselves, we hope that we too will be appreciated as this jumper is; that someone will feel about us this way and not only forgive us our frayed, misshapen bodies and characters – but will come to love us precisely for these things. We hope that tenderness, which we catch sight of in connection with a frayed old jumper, can extend its empire to us.

Holding Hands with a Small Child

You're helping walk a friend's family to kindergarten or to the local park for a picnic and your special charge is a little person – aged 3 or 4 perhaps – clutching a knitted rabbit or a favourite toy fire engine in one hand and, with the other, you. It might be something that very rarely happens in your life.

We remember from the other side as well; we're joining up with our own childhood selves; we're being big, encouraging and sweet to the little person we once were – and in part still are.

There's an unfamiliar surge of protectiveness and a revolution in one's resources of patience. And a new alertness to danger and opportunity: will those three steps be a problem? One becomes supremely careful at the kerb. A poodle being walked nearby might be charming, but for someone the same height as the dog, it contains the potential for terror. You are acutely watchful, ready at any moment to swoop in and scoop up your charge into the perfect safety of your arms.

One had forgotten how charming a child can be: the intense seriousness with which they investigate an acorn. In their company you are reconnected with how extremely interesting a puddle can be and what fascination there can be in a neighbour's rubbish bins or the wheels of parked cars.

The pleasure of the child's company is an antidote to the real (but now so familiar as to be taken for granted) errors and natural flaws of adulthood; it is the pleasure of meeting again some crucial truths – about the splendour and fascination of the world, the truth about love (and one's dormant capacity for unconditional kindness). You think, perhaps, that one day this child you are so carefully leading will themselves be your age and will do the same and have the same kind of thoughts which, at the moment, are so remote from their consciousness. And for a brief pointed time one is astonished by the utter strangeness of the course of human experience which gradually takes everyone from childhood to death.

28

Old Stone Walls

There have been decades, centuries of rain, wind, cold and sun; moss and lichen have made homes for themselves wherever they could get a foothold. Maybe this wall was being built before anyone knew the outlines of all the continents, or while the Maratha forces were winning decisive battles in the Punjab or when Napoleon was brooding on Elba. People walked past this wall every day, maybe, during the long years Queen Victoria was mourning the death of her husband. It's been around so much longer than we have. The stones it is made of were formed long before there were lizards or beetles; each one was handled by someone we will never know and whose life we can perhaps barely imagine.

You sense the impact of time, and here – for once – it is benign. Normally we think of time as bringing things to ruin. It worsens them, and it leaves them weak, shabby, broken. But here there's the pleasure of recognising a hopeful, touching truth: things can get better when they get old. The wearing effects of time can actually make something nicer. Sharp angles are softened, colours have toned down and harmonised. The old wall is a good image of ageing and endurance: it's not getting worse; strangely, it's nicer because it is older, counteracting our fears (much encouraged by the real but overstressed charms of youth and novelty) that to be old is to be worn out, unlovable, useless, ignored.

It's often the way with small pleasures: our attention is hooked before we quite know why. The charm of the wall is felt – and we may never quite work out what this thing has to say to us. And it feels normal to leave it at that. We believe that pleasure is how important meanings often introduce themselves. Behind each pleasure lies an idea, which offers a consoling or constructive perspective on existence. And it is the approach of this not yet grasped, but vaguely perceived, idea that we welcome with a feeling of joy.

29

Realising You Both Dislike the Same Popular Person

Who, and what, you dislike says something important about you. But it often feels too risky to admit that you're not much taken by someone a lot of people are pretty impressed by. It needn't be that it's a public celebrity who irritates you, it can just be someone that a lot of those you know happen to admire. You've learned to be cautious. You've had experience with negative views going wrong. You tried a sly put-down of a much-loved figure and people have reacted badly and thought you were mean or accused you of being snobbish. It's not that you don't understand the appeal at all – you just don't share it. It's a minor thing, really, of course. But the antipathy stands for something bigger: certain sides of your experience and parts of your personality have led you to this negative assessment. You can live with usually having to keep this in the shadows. But there's a cost. You slightly feel you are accommodating the limitations and misperceptions of others. You put up with others' infatuation but they won't allow you the same degree of grace and accept your honest dislike. So it's rather nice when someone else makes a move and tells you outright that they are heartily sick of this individual.

Shared antipathy creates a positive bond. One surmises that this feeling has quite deep origins and will have other manifestations. It hints positively at other shared reactions. There is some latent congruence of souls that is making itself known at this specific point.

It's lovely not having to explain or defend one's feelings in a hostile environment. It's a relief not having to politely nod in supposed agreement just to keep the peace. We don't always realise the extent to which we feel lonely in specific pockets of our inner life.

30

Feeling at Home in the Sea

Maybe you don't at first like this at all: it's been a while since you last confronted waves and felt their strange push and pull on your legs as you wade out to mid-thigh depth. You can still just see the ribbed sand on the bottom and the shadow of an occasional rock (past which a little crab may be scurrying). A mysterious strand of seaweed drifts by: you know it is safe but you have to tell yourself it is. You never quite forget the childhood fears of what might be lurking below the surface. And now you've remembered how cold it feels, even when the sea is theoretically pretty warm. You are going to have to make yourself go under. You steer well clear of a couple of splashing children and gradually dip yourself deeper into the chilling water; it seems impossible: you'll never be able to make yourself do it. And then, slowly, you let yourself sink forward; a small wave momentarily freezes your neck. And then you are in; you are used to it – safe, free and (weirdly) warm too.

You are living in another element. Walking is impossible; sitting is pointless. You bob up and down as the waves roll gently past, ducking your head under, plunging, floating on your back. And part of the background pleasure is the awareness that a slightly timid, reluctant aspect of one's nature has been enticed and coaxed to overcome its fears. A mask and snorkel let you thrive in an alien zone, while being continually supplied with the needed resources from your old, normal world. At first you can't quite believe that you can breathe; you keep on expecting to be inundated, but you are fine. The nervous instinct is calmed; your breathing becomes more natural. A tiny fish darts past. Friends' legs become bizarre, fascinating objects; the desire to suddenly grab an ankle is hard to resist. You can be yourself underwater because you have an open lifeline to the air.

Perhaps there may be many further worlds in which – with the right kind of snorkel – we can overcome the initial levels of hesitation and awkwardness. One might come to feel at home with Zen gardens, Norwegian folk music, Baroque architecture, a new relationship ...

A more adventurous part of oneself has come to life. And when you emerge, dripping and pleasantly tired, and make your way to the warm beach, you bring that part of yourself with you back from the sea, where it had been living in exile, waiting for you.

31

'Bad' Magazines

They're bad, not in the severe sense of being actually wicked and vicious, but in an intimate, personal sense: we'd be embarrassed if our acquaintances knew how much we enjoy immersing ourselves in their pages – from time to time. Other people can read them openly, just not us. You'd probably be reluctant even to buy a copy of any of them yourself – it would feel awkward to turn up at the counter clutching a copy of a magazine aimed at people of a different gender or implying a socio-economic status evidently at variance with your own or that's out of step with your general outlook. But waiting for the dentist, in the bathroom at a friend's house, or on a plane, one gets the chance to have a look without fear.

It could seem strange that you are reading them at all. You're hearing about strategies for investment in Spanish real estate, though you are just coping with paying your rent, or getting advice on what to do when a boy who has kissed you then kisses someone else at the same party, though it's many years since you've been at a social gathering where anything remotely like this could happen. You're exploring the best kind of high-speed motor boat to buy, though you are certainly never going to have to work this out for real, or getting absorbed in a critical assessment of caravan parks in North Wales with special attention to sanitary provisions, attitudes to pets and special offers for the over-60s, though you don't actually enjoy camping.

The pleasure is real, but a little puzzling. One factor that helps explain it is that we're encountering different ways of being. The lives we actually lead are tiny slivers of what is imaginatively possible. A slight shift in the past could have led to a very different kind of existence. There are lots of ways we could conceivably have turned out. There's a self who might have loved the self-reliant freedom of caravanning or relished nautical bravado. There's a stub of one's nature that with a different nurture could have evolved into a cocktail drinker or a tycoon or a devoted chess player. Hence the ambivalence. We want to be loyal to who we have become but we sense too that we contain multitudes – many alternative versions of us pursuing a shadowy existence at the back of our minds. And it's sweet to let some of them advance a little.

We're also developing areas of kinship. What we think of as a 'bad' magazine is always one that other people very much like – the circulation figures are often much higher than those of publications we consider 'good'. We're renewing the crucial thought that actually we have more in common with others than sometimes seems to be the case. In particular, it's the sense of closeness that comes from having an enjoyment in common. The anxieties that circulate around status – contempt and fear – are temporarily pacified. One can briefly commune with the worries and hopes of people whose lives are in many respects radically at odds with one's own. For a few minutes we develop a more universal capacity for sympathy. And if we keep the knowledge of this pleasure somewhere in our minds we become slightly more generous, less dismissive, versions of ourselves.

Scanning the pages of these magazines is an indulgent pleasure: you're allowed to be off the hook for a little while; you don't have to worry about the consequences; you don't have to be good. There are parts of oneself that are less clever, less controlled, less serious, less responsible, less realistic than the self one is normally required – by the demands of maturity – to be.

And an essential part of the pleasure is that we can, before too very long, close the magazine and put it away. This isn't a craving; we're not addicted. It's a small pleasure, not an overwhelming one that threatens to rob us of our freedom to put it aside.

The Song You Want to Listen to Again and Again

Maybe you felt an amazing thrill the moment you heard it; maybe you didn't think much of it at first – actually you kept on meaning to skip it; it was the next song you were really interested in. But it's grown on you. Maybe you've liked it for years but only now become obsessed with it. It might be a favourite from ages back that was linked to a specific period of your existence – you were 17 and in love, but too shy to do anything about it. You longed to dance to this song with that person – but you never did. Recently you were in a taxi and it came on the radio and you nearly cried on the way to the airport. You've looked it up and reconnected with it. Now you want to hear it all the time. And when you're not listening to it, it's still playing somewhere at the back of your mind.

You don't necessarily love everything about it. Sometimes you're waiting for the wonderful bit where they spin out a particular word – to-ni-i-i-i-ght – with the voice going up, then down, then up again in the middle in a magical way. It's such a tiny thing, a few seconds of sound, but in that space you seem to hear so much – as if everything lovely was being summed up in a wordless moment. Or there's a point when the rhythm suddenly breaks, changes pace and takes off into a soaring, pulsing section. Or when the voice and the orchestra seem to melt into each other in a brief passage of profound lyrical beauty.

We know we love it. But we don't automatically grasp quite why this song touches us so deeply and gives such pleasure. And why do we want to return to it again and again?

Our brains seem to be naturally attuned to take their cue from sounds. Gently undulating lullabies are used round the world to settle children to sleep; the murmured tones of an endearment convey love as much as the words; in a row, the bitter accents wound as much as the accusations. The mere sounds of Schubert's 'Ave Maria', for instance, seem to enfold us in tenderness. The rising passages of 'La Marseillaise' have thrilled people around the world for two centuries, even though pretty much everyone is hazy about what the words might actually mean: the sound itself reliably fires up energetic, ambitious emotions.

A song recognises something that's often missing from communication across the rest of our lives. In 'Hey Jude', the Beatles offer some fundamental advice: don't be afraid – and it's moving because the music makes us feel we're being liked as the fearful, hesitant people we are. We're being understood and sympathised with before we're being reminded that, in fact, we should make some bolder, more risky moves. It's the opposite of the unhelpful way good advice so often arrives: as a rebuke, as exasperation, as disbelief at our ineptitude. The words 'don't be afraid' can be uttered in a million different ways. But very few are actually helpful. Lennon and McCartney discovered an ideal way of getting the advice past our layers of defensive reluctance. They created an ideal emotional environment out of tone and rhythm so we're in the right frame of mind before being reminded we need to do something inherently difficult – take a risk with love.

To take a classical example, Mozart's aria 'Soave sia il vento' – blow gently, breezes – makes an impossible plea. It asks that nature let the people we love off the hook. In the specific context of the song it's asking that the boat a couple of young men are sailing in will meet with tranquil seas. But it widens to embrace all the fears we have – that those we are close to are endlessly exposed to danger and disaster that is really out of our power to prevent: the oncoming truck that veers madly across the highway, the horrific growth of cancerous cells, betrayal by others they trust, the pinions of a bike front wheel failing as they joyfully career down a lonely mountain track. And at the same time it gently insists that we have no power whatever to avert these disasters. We hope, but we are actually impotent. And therefore the song is asking us to do something profound: to appreciate properly these often very imperfect people by recognising their essential vulnerability. But it does not ask us to entertain this crucial but fearsome thought until it has coaxed us into a mood of tenderness. The melody is one of Mozart's most beautiful – gracious and sad, simple and tender. The music knows it is asking something difficult and understands we have to be settled into the right frame of mind before being confronted with a dark, but deep, thought.

We return to a song because we want to return to the state of insight the song promotes – a state that's normally fragile and, hence, fleeting. Eventually, you'll tire of it. You'll be listening to it and start to feel you wish you weren't. The words won't thrill you as they used to. It can feel a bit sad. But really it means something rather nice. You've not used it up or spoilt it by overexposure. Instead, you have fully taken possession of what you needed from it and for the time being you don't need to learn its lesson anymore. Your pleasure was the bodily signal of a benign educational experience. By a slightly basic analogy we can think of a child who for a while delights in singing the alphabet song or a little ditty that involves reciting the days of the week in the correct order. We can sense that they are taking pleasure in the acquisition of knowledge that – to them – feels important and exciting. But before too long the charm fades for them. It's because they have now fixed this fragment of wisdom in their minds. They might revert to it from time to time when the occasion demands that they recall which day follows Wednesday, but it's no longer something they sing to themselves in the back seat of the car.

Our adult needs for understanding are much more complex. What we're learning might be hard to sum up in a sentence, and might be an attitude rather than a chunk of information. But the underlying process is the same. Its demise isn't to be lamented. We have, for the time being, made its truth our own.

33

A Book that Understands You

You're turning the pages and a very strange – and very nice – thing dawns on you. This book gets you. Obviously the author (who might have died centuries back) never knew you at all. But they write as if they did. It's as if you'd confessed your secrets to them and then they'd gone off and written this work around what you'd told them – transformed, of course, into a story about people with different names or into an essay that doesn't cite your case explicitly, but might as well do so, because it's completely on target.

We never quite feel we're understood well enough even by the people who we genuinely like and who are emotionally attached to us – and who might at times be very generous, sweet or compassionate. The permafrost of loneliness persists below the surface even when things are, broadly speaking, going well enough.

The book in question might be one that speaks to millions – like the Harry Potter series. Or it could be an almost unique discovery of your own: Schiller's *Letters on the Aesthetic Education of Man,* written at the very end of the eighteenth century, with its haunting efforts to fuse a noble idealism with political realism. It could be a self-help book about sex that alights on just the thing that's troubling you. Or you might feel that *Mademoiselle de Maupin,* written by Théophile Gautier in the middle of the nineteenth century – which tells the story of a man and a woman who are both in love with the central character, the opera singer Madeleine de Maupin, and which is deeply tender towards the complexities of sexual desire – was written, by a historical miracle, exactly for you.

A book knows you by pinpointing – and taking very seriously – a major but often ignored problem that happens to be looming in your existence. For instance, when Harry Potter is with the Dursleys: the feeling of being an alien in a familiar environment. For long stretches of time Harry has to live around people who have no idea of his real nature; they never acknowledge his actual strengths and he is regarded as a contemptible freak for things that elsewhere would make him popular and important. The book is hugely alive to the feeling of not being appreciated.

We're pleased because we're encountering sympathy for things that deserve generous treatment but normally don't get it. This is what happens with Balzac's *Lost Illusions*. The central character, Lucien, does many objectively quite awful things: he's selfish, greedy, vain, he takes advantage of his friends and he makes big mistakes with his career. Balzac isn't presenting any of this as anything other than very bad. But he's deeply attentive to the forces at work around Lucien (his longing to be a success in a world stacked against him) and in him (his fear of humiliation). And it's clear Balzac very much likes this character. The darker aspects of one's character are getting a tender hearing: you have been hurt; you have hurt others. And the book says: I know.

In *Middlemarch*, George Eliot tells the story of Dorothea Brooke. She's easy to ridicule. She's got some advantages and she longs to help the world, but in fact she never does much. She makes a very unhappy marriage and wastes a large portion of her life lamenting it. In an obvious way it's all her own fault. She has plenty of chances and misses them all. It's not a self-description one is likely to be keen to avow to others. But it describes a side of many people's experience. We feel very much like this, sometimes. George Eliot isn't saying this is actually rather charming. What she offers is validation: this is what can happen to a very reasonable, well-intentioned person. It doesn't push you off the human map.

To be generously understood is nice of course – hence the pleasure – but it's a bigger thing than that. It's helpful. Because feeling alone with difficult parts of oneself increases the trouble. We're haunted by the worry that no reasonable person could feel anything but derision or contempt for our problems. We fear to share them with our friends because we anticipate bewildered rejection. The book that understands is like an ideal parent or friend who makes it acceptable to suffer in the way we do. Our weirder sorrows – or enjoyments – are recast as valid parts of human experience, which can be met with sympathy and kindness.

34

Crying Cathartically over the Death of a Fictional Character

We know they're not real. They never were alive so they can't actually have died at all. Yet hearing about their imagined end is hugely affecting. If the circumstances are sufficiently private – lying on the bed in a dressing-gown on Sunday afternoon with the book open in a shaft of sunlight – one might frown, the upper lip puckers, the eyes are intensely shut and the sobbing starts. The tears are running down one's cheek. And when it's over we feel deeply calm and rather happy. But unlike the real versions of death, we don't keep on being grimly struck by the return of the terrible fact: they are dead. We can anyway just skip back a few pages and there they are again, as much alive as they ever were. But why do we actually enjoy crying over their death?

In Anthony Trollope's Palliser series – written in the second half of the nineteenth century – we live with his central character Glencora Palliser though six long books. She was so nice; she suffered a lot in her long marriage but eventually learned to love her difficult husband. She was funny and naughty and kind. By the last novel she is still only in her forties, but she's very ill. Perhaps it's her heart; perhaps it's cancer – Trollope doesn't go into detail. Her children are stumbling towards adulthood and are very much in need of her; their father, though deeply loving, is distant, stern and preoccupied with his political career. Glencora was a slightly wild girl who evolved into an ideal mother. She never forgot her own past unhappiness, when she was disappointed in an early relationship – and that constant awareness is a source of her tenderness towards her children; she is warm, forgiving and desperate to shield them from the worst consequences of their own mistakes. So, when she dies, we're witnessing the loss of this lovely quality.

Genuinely lovely things – the things the character has reminded us we deeply need and admire – often seem quite weak in the world. There are more powerful forces: a mother's love can't beat cancer; a teasing, warm, funny mind is still enshrined in a horribly vulnerable case of flesh. We are crying, in part because we are recognising ourselves as very strange sorts of entities, destined to be most attached to things that are frighteningly transient. For a moment we are feeling justifiably sorry for ourselves that this is so. And, sadly, it's not just an imaginary person in a book who has died. The very thing we've come to love in them, and whose loss we mourn, has been damaged, even 'killed', by us, from time to time in ourselves. We've been sometimes sour and righteous and unyielding. We've been at odds with and disloyal to the lovely things about this person. And we're sorry.

It's very touching, too, to read of the death of a young Russian soldier, Petya Rostov, which occurs near the end of Tolstoy's *War and Peace*. He's a rather minor character, the young brother of Nikolai and Natasha, who figure much more prominently. His death occurs towards the end of the French campaign of 1812 in Russia. Moscow has already burned, the French armies are in desperate retreat westwards through the snow and blizzards. They are being chased by Cossack troops accompanied by a few officers from the regular army. Amongst them – the most junior of subalterns – is Petya. He's so young, perhaps just 16. He's on the threshold of life. He is so desperate to join in and do something to help his country. He's forthright and eager and loyal. Then in the night he gets caught in sniper fire and is fatally wounded. But what's most moving is that another character, Dolokhov, who is otherwise a rather brutish man, tries to shield him and feels the horror of this young life being destroyed and weeps beside him in the snow. It's a high point of Tolstoy's artistry to give this tender role to Dolokhov. Because this tough individual, who is generally indifferent to the suffering of others, is a version of us, the reader. We're not thuggish like him, but in our own ways we are often wrapped up in a cloak of indifference. We've become hardened, we've had to filter out so much. We're weeping not simply for the death of this character, but for an elemental fact that's being portrayed through Petya: the idiotic randomness of death.

We're being brought up against how we would feel if some much altered (but emotionally connected) version of this did occur in our lives. No one deserves to die. Yet anyone's life can be cut off in a moment. We are being resensitised, by a made-up story, to a profound fact. And via that we are, ideally, reactivated in an important area of appreciation. Petya's parents and brother and sister were often exasperated by him; he wasn't a perfect person. He skipped his homework; he was a bit full of himself; he had some silly ideas. But these seem – after the bullet – such minor things. Death reorganises our priorities; it changes our scale of assessment. His parents would give anything to have him be disobedient or arrogant again, so long as he was back.

We're weeping not simply about the demise of a fictional character, we're crying in acknowledgement of a painful truth. We may only realise the full extent of our love for people too late. We are being agonisingly alerted not just to a possible loss, but to a failure of our own. In crying, we are taking the warning to heart and wishing, if only we could, to properly love the desperately imperfect people at the centre of our lives while there is still time.

Another side of our tears comes into focus around the death of a dog, Argos, recounted in the ancient story of *The Odyssey* – which tells of the long wandering of Ulysses on his journey from the siege of Troy back to his troubled home in Ithaca. Ulysses is the king of the small island but when he gets back he's alone and in disguise. He's been away for 20 years. He looks like a worn-out old beggar. Almost everyone has long ago given him up for dead. There's no happy, wonderful reception for him. He's alone and his house is filled with arrogant, boorish rivals who want to claim his wife and seize his kingdom. But at this grim moment, when he's facing these problems, something wonderful happens. Argos, his old hunting dog, approaches. He's diseased and his coat is infested with lice. He had been waiting and watching for his master's return and now he recognises him, and a deep love and joy give him the strength to rouse himself and go to greet him. But the effort is too much. It's his last quietly heroic act. And he dies.

'Argos passed into the darkness of death, now that he had fulfilled his destiny of faith and seen his master once more.' *The Odyssey*, Book 17

The death of Argos can be so moving because through him we're being reconnected with our own past suffering. We've lost so many things that were important to us: childhood innocence, a former relationship, an avenue of trust, a level of confidence that got punctured. Like him, we were always watching for this return. We find echoes of all these things in the fate of Argos. But with this one crucial difference. What he loved came back. For us it never will, because it never can. It is ourselves we are weeping for.

The tears are a pleasure because we know we're responding rightly – we are experiencing the generosity in ourselves that responds so warmly, so intensely, to the imagined situation. We are crying because, in our deeply muddled and often very difficult lives, in which we have every reason to think ill of ourselves, we are suddenly reminded of our own remarkable, real and often hidden capacity for pure goodness.

Pleasant Exhaustion after a Productive Day

It's 9.45 pm. You put in an extra, late spurt – for supper you had a toasted sandwich at your desk, brushing the occasional crumb from the keyboard while you kept at it. It was difficult. But now it's done. You've made the progress you'd hoped to. Probably, it will all start again in the morning, but you'll be working off a solid base – it won't be the familiar scramble to catch up.

You're worn out. You had to make yourself stick at it – but now you're glad you did. There's a gentle ache in the middle of your back. You yawn and turn your neck from side to side; you stretch round and try to massage an awkward spot below your left shoulder blade. In a while you'll need to head off to bed – but not just yet. It's nice to linger and spin out the moment of repletion. It's lovely to saunter about and make a cup of tea or let some wine gurgle from the bottle into a glass. You might flick indifferently through the newspaper. You can't get engaged: your brain has done its work and shies away from any further effort.

The pleasure we feel after a good but hard day's work is linked to a positive experience of willpower. It was tempting to break off; you could have put it off until tomorrow (you've often done that in the past); you could have become distracted (which is achingly familiar); you could have stayed physically at your desk but actually been fantasising about glamorous apartments in New York or finding out what a television personality is up to at the moment. But you didn't. You stuck with the big thing.

It's also to do with a sense of mastery: in anticipation we slightly feared the task. But we got on top of this tricky thing and we tamed it. There were points when it felt we might not: it was too difficult; a solution seemed elusive; there were too many things we were trying to get right at the same time; a mass of details needed to be reduced to a simple, coherent shape – though it wasn't at all obvious what this could be. An awkward email needed a tactful but firm response; a refusal had to be delivered without a sting; a criticism needed to be put forward delicately but very clearly. A hunch had to be turned into a proposal – and there's always a difficult point at which what had, from a distance, seemed like a good idea starts to look much less impressive close up, yet it was onto something ... only what exactly? Maybe you had to revise a report and you dreaded unpicking work you had already done and facing the same old issues once again. We've been labouring against the normal forces of disintegration. Things that were scattered and messy have been brought together, harmonised, tidied up, elucidated. We've done something fundamental. We've held back the tide of chaos.

The pleasure of a long productive day hints at a bigger theme. It's not simply about this moment and the particular tasks we've polished off. It's a promise that other problems can be faced as well. We're reminded of a capacity within ourselves to deal with difficulties, to get on top of challenges and to keep going until they are under control. We're seeing in ourselves an antidote to the fear of drifting. We naturally worry we'll be swamped by demands; we know our own unfortunate tendency to let things fester. But right now, we're conscious of something else. We're capable of rousing ourselves, of focus and of sustained effort. We can stick with something difficult and keep going through the temptations to break off and seek distraction. We've been just a little bit heroic and we know it and it feels nice.

Exhaustion is – all too often – a reason to have to give up because one's strength has failed too soon. The brain starts to melt when really we should be getting on with a big task; the mind is worn out while the problem remains unsolved. Instead, now, we're experiencing honourable or worthy tiredness. Instead of getting annoyed with ourselves for lacking energy, our pleasant tiredness feels like the natural and just reward for our labours. It's setting us up for a good night's sleep.

36
Old Photos of One's Parents

She is on a beach in a one-piece bathing suit, grinning wildly, looking deeply proud of something, standing next to a boy you don't recognise – her cousin Kenneth? It's your mother aged maybe 7 or 8 (and a half it must be, because her birthday is in December and she never went to the other side of the world until she was 23 to spend a year teaching at a school in Brisbane). You try to work out the year the photo would have been taken. While she was making sandcastles – which she still likes to do with your little niece – and splashing her friends, were students throwing rocks at the police in the side streets of Paris? At that exact time, were NASA scientists racing to sort out a problem with the booster rockets for the first moon landing which would occur that autumn? (It's a family story that she was allowed to stay up late to watch it live on television.) What was it like to be alive then and to feel these events not as history but simply as the vague current background to a summer holiday by the sea?

In another picture, your father looks unfeasibly slender, but his shoulders, typically, are slightly hunched. He's sitting outside a bar – it looks like somewhere in Venice – with strange masses of chestnut hair. Even when he had it he couldn't control it. Who could have taken this picture? You should ask him sometime, though conversations with him aren't necessarily your favourite thing right now. It must have been years before he met your mother because in their wedding photos he's already put on weight and his hairline has started to move. Was he still studying? Was he going out with someone? You remember your mother asking about someone called Sandra and your father saying 'I really can't bear to find out how she's getting on' – and then being a bit silent. But he often lapses into silence so it's hard to know if it's significant. Yet in the photo he looks eager and engaged, as if there's something witty he's about to say.

Our parents are – in a certain sense – amongst the people we know best in the world. We passed so long in their company. We've had far more meals with them than their best friends have. We know them as we know few others: we've seen them in their seven o'clock in the morning guise, we've seen them anxious and occasionally furious, we've been cradled in their arms, we've seen their underwear drawer and their toenails, and we are expert judges of their ability to erect a tent or make a dish of macaroni cheese.

But looking at the photos we realise that in other ways we hardly know them at all. What was it actually like to be them? If you could know them at the same age, would you like them? Would you feel a strange kinship? And, today, what are they like alone with their friends? What parts of their character have you maybe not seen properly yet?

The pleasure, below the surface, is of an increase in love. Inevitably, there has to be plenty about a parent that is irksome – it's scarcely possible to grow up without feeling in some ways let down by one's parents. It's not exclusively their fault – especially if they have tried quite hard to be good parents to us. It's rather that as we grow they can't live up to the admiring, passionate love we once had for them. The person who – when we were 6 – appeared majestic, wise, endlessly funny and bountiful will in time be revealed as fussy, intermittently slothful and hyperactive; they will be seen to harbour eccentric preoccupations; they will embarrass us; they will get baffled by trivial problems; at crucial moments they will fail us in profound ways – entirely without meaning to.

The photos make us realise something we find almost impossible to grasp when we are children: our parents' lives weren't mainly about us. They didn't spend their entire existence gearing up for us. In these pictures they had no idea whatever of what would happen in the future. You were raised by a girl with a naughty smirk and a shy young man – not by perfectly mature adults who unaccountably got some key things wrong. Guided by these images we become – if only for a little while – more forgiving and more accommodating towards these nice, strange people who happen to have given us our lives.

One day, perhaps, another person will look at a photo of you – a photo whose meaning to you is transparent and which vividly evokes every detail of the remembered experience – and feel the same kind of tender, puzzled curiosity. And perhaps they will wonder, in their turn, what their mother or father was like when they were young and who they really are in the full, complex expanse of their being?

Whispering in Bed in the Dark

You can't even see each other's noses, though they are just a few inches apart. The darkness isn't separating you, it's bringing you together. Theoretically it shouldn't really matter – as far as the wider world is concerned you are just as secluded in the brightly lit kitchen. But having the lights out reassures a more primitive anxiety: if we can see, we can be seen. It's the same reason why whispering feels necessary: it intensifies the atmosphere of seclusion.

The ancient philosopher Diogenes, who made his home in a disused wine barrel in a main street of Athens, took the view that if you are willing to do something in private you should have the courage to do it in public too (masturbation was one of his favourite topics of intellectual discourse). He was onto something, but also missing something important: deep privacy is genuinely liberating. It's actually rather nice that we are concerned to present a more restrained, adult and reasonable face to the world. But, it's true, we're not revealing the whole of who we are. And this is what gives whispering in the dark its special place in our lives. We have all the liberating benefits of being alone – but we are also with another person.

The darkness also marks an important separation from the rest of the day. The things that occupied you no longer feel relevant – for a while, anyway. Our feelings and thoughts are so liable to be dominated by the external demands of life. It's quite difficult to switch them off. We need the assistance of big, external cues. In the dark, other senses come to the fore. Every detail of the voice becomes more noticeable. Nothing significant is being discussed but something significant is happening.

Sometimes you use pet names: Lillybilly and Billylilly, Blinker and Stinker. They can sound silly if they're pronounced in the middle of the day. But now they help us shed, strategically and briefly, major parts of our lives – so that other key things about us can get a chance to shine. Lillybilly isn't pursuing a career in finance; Stinker isn't a vigorous logical reasoner; Billylilly doesn't care whose turn it is to stack the dishwasher; Blinker doesn't know what a mortgage is. Quite possibly no one in the world knows you use them. They set you apart. They mark us out (at the moment) as 'us', quite different from all of 'them'. No one can overhear anyway, but whispering feels natural: you are sharing a deep secret.

You want to giggle; you feel playful. You say silly things that normally you'd censor. You can tell someone you love them. It often becomes tricky to do this at other times. Our practical, responsible, ambitious and anxious selves find it increasingly hard to make this assertion: the idea of love gets awkwardly caught up in minor irritations and differences of opinion. It can feel too tricky to be emotionally vulnerable (because to tell someone you love them is to risk them not responding with adequate warmth). But now it's different. The complicating factors don't matter just at the moment. So you can be tender and open without so much fear.

You are joining forces with your childhood self. When you were little you loved to go exploring down to the bottom of the bed – your mother pretended to not know what could be down there, she'd pat you and wonder out loud: 'What's this big lump? Could it be a pillow? No, it's a bit hard for a pillow (another vigorous pat). I hope it's not a crocodile escaped from the zoo.' And you'd almost believe she might mean it – though really her mind was mainly on the fact that the bed would need to be remade and that if you got too excited you wouldn't get to sleep. You had the idea it would be nice to sleep upside down, with your head where your feet would normally be – but it's actually not very nice after about a minute.

There were other times you pulled the blankets over your head and the normal arrangements of the world no longer applied: you could imagine you lived in an igloo or were a baby beaver safe in a little house on the dam in the middle of a pond; you could be a snail inside its shell. Or you could be a pirate with a sword, a cruel laugh and lots of captives, all tied up.

When your cousins came to stay you used to all try to get under the covers together in your pyjamas after brushing your teeth – four was a lovely squeeze – until an adult came in and told everyone to go to their own beds and mattresses. One of those times a cousin told you all what 'fuck' means – though she didn't get it quite right.

You explore a hip bone or a thigh. Your toes touch. It's not overtly sexual, just at the moment, though you might get there later. There are other pleasures – less urgent – but just as real that occupy us now.

Cypress Trees

You don't often pay much attention to trees, but you always like it when you do. And a cypress might only catch your eye very occasionally. There was one in your aunt's garden, but she moved house a few years ago. You have a hazy memory of a scene you felt was rather lovely in a film – it was on a hillside somewhere Mediterranean (was it set in Malta?) and in the background there was a hillside with some cypress trees. And strangely it's the background that's stuck in your mind all these years. And once you went to an old hotel that had a terrace with a row of cypress trees in large stone basins. You always had a soft spot for cypress trees, but you haven't thought much about it.

They are very distinctive entities. The pencil, or Tuscan evergreen cypress, doesn't spread itself out. Sometimes you might feel they are shy. At others times the idea of being aloof comes to mind. They are very private: there's the dark intensity to their colouring. They do well in graveyards. The sides form themselves into long upright curves but the top tends to be jagged. Once you start looking carefully you find it's quite hard to identify each branch and every little irregularity of the shape of one individual tree. It's especially nice when you see a cluster of them on the horizon jutting into a clear blue sky.

The enjoyment of seeing a cypress tree isn't just to do with how nice they look. There's also a pleasure of identification: the sense that despite all the obvious differences the tree has something to teach us – it is a living sermon on endurance.

They survive a very long time. A large one could have been around when the Third Estate took the Tennis Court Oath and unwittingly set the events of the French Revolution in motion; it may have suffered in the 'great winter' of 1708–9, the worst of its immensely long life. Its bark was probably thickening and it was just getting going when Florentine bankers were funding the Renaissance.

And any particular tree you happen to come across could well have hundreds of years still to live. When we're in a nursing home doing a jigsaw, it will be doing fine. It could still be around when there are cities in Antarctica, when the first human–robot wedding is celebrated, when Mars becomes self-governing.

A tree can't flee or alter its environment. It is stuck in the single place where it was planted or where the seed happened to fall into a little crevice. Naturally, we're attracted to the idea of being able to alter our condition, but sometimes we just have to put up with difficulties. We're not being pathetic or weak. Our bigger commitments tie us to a situation. Or we're facing things that – like a broken leg, a downturn in the economy or the fact of ageing – we don't have the power to do anything much about. We're stuck with something and then ideally we'd be more like the cypress, clinging on, keeping going. They are so patient. They put up with so much.

They manage to grow well in places that don't look especially hospitable – the hillside seems stony and dry, the wind howls, the sun is intense. But they somehow extract enough moisture from the soil. They resist summer fires and renew themselves in the charred landscape. They are evergreen – they don't change with the seasons. What's happening outside doesn't alter what's happening inside them. They grow very slowly, but they do grow; maturation takes so long.

One could imagine a micro-pilgrimage – undertaken perhaps on a weekly basis – to visit a cypress tree and to reconnect with the fragment of wisdom it enshrines. Or it might be wise to place a photo of a cypress at a strategic place where you tend to get agitated and experience conflict: in the kitchen, near the bathroom door through which, in moments of un-cypress-like desperation, you have a habit of shouting at the person on the other side. And where a glance at its compact form might transmit to you, in a moment of need, a little of its noble endurance.

News of a Scientific Discovery

If you don't have much day-to-day involvement with the world of science, it can still be charming to come across a news item reporting a breakthrough in pure research – and the fact that the details of the story are pretty much incomprehensible somehow doesn't seem to matter. A dust cloud has been detected in the Lagoon nebula; progress is being made in understanding the neural networks in the brains of fish; the existence of a particular subatomic particle has been confirmed; or scientists have discovered that at ultra-low temperatures chemicals can react with each other at much greater distances than is possible at room temperature.

The announcement of these scientific breakthroughs occurs side by side with the regular dramas of the news: a government policy adviser has accidentally sent a nude photo of themselves to the leader of the opposition; a badly decomposed corpse has been found in a Scottish loch; the German economy is not doing what it was expected to do; a woman in Ohio has the world's largest collection of umbrellas. All the normal things are happening. And somewhere in the background people have been quietly finding out about galactic dust and the neural processing of carp and herrings.

We might not really grasp the special meaning of these discoveries. And we're not necessarily imagining possible practical applications. But there seems to be a distinctive pleasure circulating around them, which is linked to a powerful, but nebulous, idea: progress.

The stories are describing recent, tiny steps in a vast and very long process. It's taken us very slowly and gradually from thinking that thunder was the rage of a furious being in the sky to recognising that it is a sound produced by the rapid thermal expansion of the air caused by an electrical discharge; or from thinking that the heart is the seat of the emotions to the view that it is a pump. And more generally from the sense that nature is a dark mystery to the view that everything can be clearly explained if only we investigate it properly. The small piece of scientific news is a point of contact with the grand vision of the advancement of understanding, the rolling back of superstition and truth triumphing over error.

Little phrases of the news items are especially touching: 'at a research laboratory in Minnesota ...', 'Professor Emilius and her team ...', 'researchers from a network of over one hundred universities ...' They imply devoted, careful people spending years working together towards these discoveries. These weren't strokes of luck. They weren't random. They were planned. There were massive banks of delicate instruments, fiendish calculations, logically constructed hypotheses and systematic experimentation. Huge quantities of brainpower were trained on very specific problems. We're not just pleased at these specific little increments of human knowledge, we're responding to the larger theme of organised intelligent effort which lies behind them. We're struck by the grandeur of the collective effort, the strategic patience and the successful pitting of intelligence against a mystery.

We may not, in all honesty, care very deeply about how fish process visual information or what happens to Barium at -270 degrees Celsius. But news of scientific advancement is sweet because it edges into our minds the idea of such carefully arranged progress occurring in other areas of human life. We can pleasantly imagine the same kind of highly structured effort being applied to issues closer to the centre of our own lives. Rather than a billion euro budget, 2,000 researchers and a large chunk of a Swiss valley being devoted to working out what's going on inside atoms, we can imagine equally large-scale endeavours devoted to working out what's going on inside our relationships. There would be just as big a concerted drive with as many people employed in carefully defined research teams, splitting the problem into tiny sections (here is the team who focus exclusively on Sunday evening; this team is working on couples and money, this one is tackling sex). Their distinctive efforts won't get lost because they are all part of a vast, beautifully designed programme. For almost all time up to very recently we were totally in the dark about physical entities. It seemed impossible ever to make sense of it. Now the problem is largely understood. And other areas, too, could yield.

Over many years in large-scale controlled experiments, thousands of highly trained people might pore over tiny details (the lip curl, the indignant stare, fear conditioning and amygdala activity). For a while the discoveries would seem abstract and only of theoretical interest. But they'd gradually unravel the confusions in our lives and their insights would one day lead to the design of conflict-inhibiting kitchens and highly accurate prognostic tools for assessing potential partners; and eventually simplified versions of their insights could be written into colourful textbooks designed to win the attention of lively 7-year-olds.

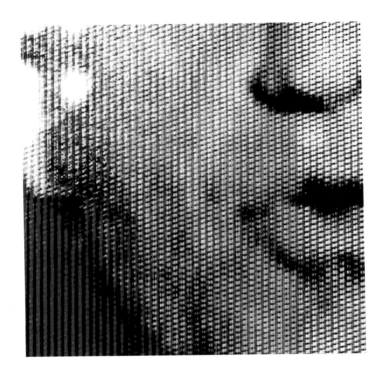

40

Feeling Someone Else
Is So Wrong

Often we're in search of agreement. It's very nice when someone wholeheartedly agrees with something we've said, especially when we thought they'd be against us.

But there's also special satisfaction when someone is not just slightly out in what they say; they're not just exploring an interesting idea you don't particularly happen to agree with or advancing a plausible-sounding, but actually mistaken, hypothesis. Over dinner or listening to the radio in the car, we're finally in the company of someone who is deeply, wildly, plainly wrong.

It could happen around some conflicted bit of political history or some key problem of modern life: maybe they said that Margaret Thatcher was the best British leader of the twentieth century or that she was the worst. Maybe they're saying that global warming is a conspiracy of left-wing scientists or that before long cruise ships will be docking in Central Park. They could be insisting that everything built since 1945 is ugly or that we are living in the golden age of architecture; that capitalism has brought the world to its knees or that it is the most successful economic system ever devised. Just now, the final truth of the issue doesn't matter. We get excited because – in our eyes – what they're saying is monstrously in error. We feel we're totally in the right and they are totally wrong.

It's tempting to say we simply can't believe they are actually saying this. But behind the scenes (and without quite realising it) we've been waiting for someone to come along and assert just this particular form of stupidity. We've entertained it in our own heads as a strikingly absurd option. We've maybe made rapid mental portraits of the sort of person who would say this.

One aspect of the pleasure is linked to the clear appreciation we get – by contrast – of our own wisdom and intelligence. There is a thrilling coiling of intellectual energy as one listens to their folly. Pretty often we're unsure of what we think. Across a wide range of topics we're conscious of our own ignorance. We struggle every day with issues that we don't fully understand. But now their antithetic stance brings our own happy knowledge and insight to the fore. They make us slightly brilliant.

The world starts to divide: there are those (like you) who are right and there are others (like this individual) who are sunk in confusion. So often we are dealing in nuance and ambiguity; so frequently we have to accommodate the notion that there's something to be said on the other side; but now there's an end to that. We experience the satisfaction of inhabiting a simpler, clearer world.

This pleasure is also linked to personal history. Years ago there was a person who loomed large in your life who took this kind of view: a parent, an unsympathetic teacher, an overbearing individual you were at college with. They used to spout things along these lines. And at that time you couldn't hold your own. But now you can. Then you felt they were somehow totally mistaken, but you couldn't match their confident assertions.

You're not angry now – there's no longer any fear or rage or hatred. But there's a pleasant feeling of meeting again a representative of this deeply wrong style of thought, when now you are strong and skilled enough to stand up to it perfectly. The terrors of the past are behind you. Now you can cope – and more than that. You can come back the way you always wished you could.

One particularly charming and special instance of the pleasure occurs when this person is advocating an idea we actually used to believe in ourselves. You once thought as they do, but life, experience, better information or clearer thinking have – you feel sure – shown you the large error of your former conviction. And this person has clearly failed to take the crucial steps you have.

At such a moment, we get a compelling sense of our own cognitive progress. (The way a child who is currently struggling with multiplication looks pityingly on a young sibling who still has to ask what number comes after seven.) We're actually thrilling in our own case to the creed of the Enlightenment: that information and reason could lead humanity as a whole to the truth. That all disagreement is misunderstanding. Teaching will always triumph over mistakes. Ideally we should not so much try to put this person right, or despise them for their misguided mentality, as thank them for the pleasing insight they have – quite inadvertently – alerted us to.

And, to be painfully honest, it is a pleasure which we have to admit we will inevitably, from time to time, provide for others to whom our own cherished beliefs or occasional stray assertions will offer the perfect foil for their own convictions and for whom we will be the ideal, perfect idiot.

41

The Teasing of Old Friends

It's a particular sign of friendship that people know they can tease you – and that, even when there is a slight sting to their remarks, you rather like it. They email a photo of a gorilla that does slightly resemble you when you are fed up about something. If you're catching a flight with them they suggest arriving five hours early (or maybe the night before), knowing your tendency to panic about being late; they secretly count the number of times you use a particular word and congratulate you after an hour for only having said 'actually' 23 times. They like making sly reminders of old follies – they don't let you forget about the summer when you were sure you were going to live in a hut in Norway and grow your own vegetables (though you've ended up working in marketing for a major office supply firm and get your potatoes from the local supermarket).

At its best, teasing allows genuinely difficult issues to be raised in an atmosphere of affection. Yes, you're having an extra glass of wine, as you always seem to do. You do tend to predictably spin off into a rant on a strange range of topics: Japanese aesthetics, snowboarding, the future of China or the right way to make scrambled eggs. Your friends know exactly how to prod you into a state of high agitation. They are gently – and usefully – educating you in the distorted aspects of your own preoccupations; a lesson is being delivered in the form of a joke, when they start laughing just when you thought you were about to arrive at the clinching point and that you would, finally, persuade them of your superior wisdom on these matters.

The crucial background is that the teasing friend has known all about these sides of you for ages and has stuck with you and is very fond of you. It can sound like such a little thing: they know my faults and they like me anyway. But really it's a lovely thing – and much too rare.

So often a useful point can't get through to us because we experience it as a criticism. We feel it is part of the case being made against us. It is a reason why we can't be loved. And so we want, if at all possible, to shut it out of our minds or turn our own frustration with ourselves against the person reminding us of an unpalatable truth. It's a key problem of life: we reject difficult but important knowledge because it comes wrapped in the wrong way. The old friend covers their insight in kindness and fun and so we may be able to acknowledge – in the guise of a tease – things we've savagely repudiated when we sensed scorn or disappointment in the delivery.

Teasing works because the old friend knows you are not going to fall apart. They could wound you. They know how to deeply distress you and deliberately make sure not to. They don't bluntly accuse you of having been awful to an ex (though you now recognise you were) or of having mucked up a portion of your career (which you never forget for a moment). The surrounding goodwill is large and well-established, the touch is light; the paws are velveted. That's what it is to feel at the same time known and liked.

So often we despair of the two – knowledge and love – being united. It feels as if we can only secure the goodwill of others by carefully editing our self-presentation and keeping the less admirable aspects of our characters hidden. Or we feel that we can be known only at the price of being condemned: if they saw the darker corners of who

I am, no one could like me. The teasing old friend finds the small, wonderful intersection: they see us as we really are and yet they love us.

And at the heart of it there's an unspoken invitation to reciprocate. It's not one-sided: you know how to tease them back and you know that's a pleasure for them too.

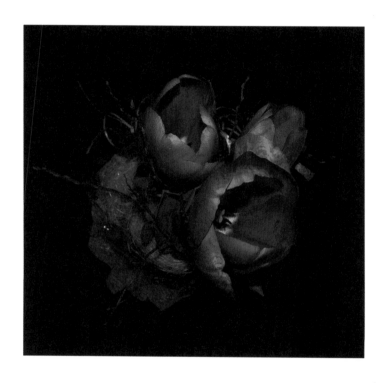

42

Getting over a Row

It was horrendous while it was going on. You said some awful things – though you were pushed so hard. You slammed a door. They shouted. You felt angry with them and angry with yourself. You felt ashamed of yourself and yet sure it was their fault. You wanted to force them to see your point. You got stubborn and cold; you weren't going to budge. Why should you apologise – they're the one who should be saying sorry. You should apologise but it will only make them feel they were right – which they're not. Maybe this is the end. Perhaps we're no good together. Our inherited fantasy of the ideal relationship focuses on harmony. Rows expose areas of hostility and true fissures in the ideal of togetherness. But in their aftermath – as one cools down – various small pleasures emerge.

One compensating satisfaction is realising you can only say such things to someone you are actually very close to. The capacity to be horrible to your partner is a strange – but genuine – feature of love. A relationship has to include the madder, more unreasonable parts of ourselves. If I can be overtly angry with you, it's because you have made me feel safe enough to be so. I never slam a door at work, I never tell a colleague to their face I think they are a bastard or a bitch, but that's not because I like them better than you, it's because those relationships are wrapped up in layers of repression and fear – I'd lose my job, or I'd become an outcast in the office. The strange thing is, I am petulant and at times nasty around you because you have reassured me so much. I let the guard down and the more troubled parts of me feel safe enough to emerge. It's sometimes only after a couple has made a public commitment to each other, when they've openly stated that they mean to stay together through thick and thin, that the most blazing and lacerating rows actually start to happen. The natural instinct is to think we've made a terrible mistake getting together. But a deeper part of the explanation of why we're so upset is strangely positive.

There's also a satisfaction in having cleared the air. Between you, you have given voice (admittedly in a rather harsh way) to some things that were festering in the dark. It took a lot of emotional upheaval to state them. But now they are in the open. And potentially you can start to look at them in a slightly more sane and measured way. It's a relief – at last – to be looking properly at a troublesome issue.

And sometimes it happens that a row is the turbulent passage to a deeper reconciliation. It was important for the two of you to be able to say these difficult, genuinely painful and hurtful things to one another. By foregrounding for a while the points of conflict, you inadvertently set up the conditions for remembering the larger areas of closeness. You remember that they are very nice in other ways – the conflict occupies a smaller place in your mind.

There are also, perhaps, the small pleasures of forgiving and of being forgiven. We're not simply forgetting. The things that were done and said are still vivid, but they come to be seen in a larger, more benign and less frightening way. Forgiveness mainly comes from recognising the background of stress, worry and fear that frames the person's behaviour. They were awful to you, but the reasons they were awful might have very little to do with you. In fact, the shouting, the swearing, the cold stares or the looks of disgust are fuelled by external factors – some of them perhaps originating long before this person came into your life. You are only the unfortunate lightning rod their anger flashes down on. We like forgiving, because, at its best, it means understanding better why this person got so upset – and when one understands, it feel less personally offensive. And similarly, being forgiven is nice when it implies that one's problems are better grasped. We're saying to each other, in effect: I've remembered now how hard it is to be you, therefore I'm less personally affronted by your conduct.

Particularly difficult rows bring to light areas of opposition that, quite possibly, just can't be resolved. You might, for instance, have thought you could run a business together, but a series of bruising rows convinces you that it's just not going to work. You used to always go to one person's parents at the weekend, but it's causing huge conflicts. You are turned off by some areas of sexuality that are important to your partner.

Getting over a row means gradually realising – with quiet satisfaction – you can cope with a problem that you can't solve directly. We'll give up trying to be a couple in this particular area. It's not what either of us would have ideally wanted. But we'll be OK. The nature of the relationship evolves slightly. From now on, maybe we won't go to the supermarket together; it will be a solo performance from now on at family gatherings – the in-laws will think it's odd but we'll survive that. We'll adjust the boundaries of our joined life.

Conflict is a pretty much unavoidable part of living closely with another person and being involved in big, complicated mutual undertakings. But we're all right now and that's nice – until the next time.

Planning the Ideal Routine

It's enjoyable to sit with a big sheet of paper and map out what the best arrangement for a typical day or week would be for you. It's not a fantasy – you're not day-dreaming about a roster of lovers or the ideal time for the butler to bring the cocktail tray. The ideal routine is closely aligned with your actual life: it just tries to set out a good way of organising the things you are already involved in.

The background to the pleasure is our familiar awareness of a day going badly wrong. We get in a panic because we end up with four things all needing to be done at once – in the next five minutes, you have to have a shower, pick up some things from the dry-cleaners, pay three bills on-line and finish a report for work. Life is slipping away, yet we're not using the time we have wisely. The hope – enshrined in the notion of an ideal schedule – is that we'd discover that in fact we do have enough time, if only we can learn to use it wisely.

It's nice just to be clear about what the recurrent things actually are and to assign each one a distinct slot on a daily or weekly basis. The chaotic multiplicity of being very busy starts to devolve into a limited set of repeatable tasks. A starting point might be the overt demands of pretty much every day: when to get up, when to go to bed, a time to catch up on correspondence, what time to have supper or when to fit in some exercise.

But a crucial part of the charm is making definite space for things that don't typically get included in a to-do list.

There's the inclusion of apparently eccentric things – 10.35 am, have a nap; 3.00 pm, think of someone you dislike and for two minutes imagine being them; 6.55 pm, look at a photo of a skull and think about the fact that you will die. There's a specific slot for things that don't normally feel like they should be planned for: stare out of the window, eat a nectarine. One might plan a specific 'Marcus Aurelius moment' (taking up a suggestion from the stoic Roman Emperor: while brushing your teeth, mentally run through a list of people you are grateful to and recall the good they have done you).

Taking an overview of a week or a month, we can also mark out times for ritual occasions. Tuesdays, 11.45 pm, go for a walk, think about a specific area of childhood: this coming week, aged 12, the year you changed schools; what were you like then? What did you care about? What was tricky? What went well? Two weeks' time: 13–15, the early stage of adolescence.

All these activities can sound odd when stated on an agenda – but that's not because they are unimportant or unworthy of intelligent consideration. It's just because, unfortunately, their contribution to a proper life hasn't as yet been fully appreciated or collectively admitted.

A key question is how much time should you assign to any one thing? Some tricky tasks lose their sting if we break them into brief chunks: if you find domestic accounts annoying you, just slip in one painful thing at a time. The schedule tells you – pay two bills online (11 minutes) prior to a snack of salted biscuits and a wedge of Emmental. We're envisaging a release from procrastination. And it can also help us with things we like but that get distressing if we spend too long on them. The routine says: 2.15 pm, read the newspaper or scan a news website – but at 2.30 pm you have to go on to doing the laundry or working on a review of the corporate recruitment strategy. It's lovely to catch up on what's happening in the world, but if you spend 56 minutes on it, you start to feel you're wasting your life; the routine offers to protect you from your own annoying tendencies.

A charming promise of a routine is that many more things will become habits. You won't have to decide to do them and summon a special burst of willpower: after the first dozen times they start to become semi-automatic. The day begins to flow. You're not always prodding and badgering yourself to get on with what you should be doing.

The pleasure of thinking through the ideal schedule takes issue with the Romantic idea that what's organised, planned and recurrent can't also be lovely. The Romantic imagination likes to peg enjoyment to what's rare and unexpected, to what happens on the spur of the moment and to the chance turn of events. It's not entirely wrong. Obviously, sometimes, sweet and fun things are spontaneous and unexpected. But it fosters an unfortunate negative attitude towards the expected and pre-booked; it looks down on the carefully arranged diary. But now we are reminding ourselves of another, though less widely recognised, delight: the pleasing vision of life organised, sorted – and carefully timetabled and mapped out with colour-coded pencils.

You are not necessarily going to stick to it in every detail, and you might revise it tomorrow – or you might only put a sliver of it into action. But the thought of the ideal routine is helping one understand a little better what one needs to become a slightly better, more organised, productive and calm version of oneself.

Finally Gaining the Respect of a Previously Suspicious Colleague

You recently started a new job and there was a colleague who gave you a hard time. Or perhaps a new person has come in to a project to work alongside you, or now you are reporting to someone you haven't worked with before. Admittedly they haven't been overtly hostile or even impolite. But you could sense they didn't as yet really believe in you. There was something slightly frosty about their manner. They didn't pay much attention when you presented at a meeting; their emails were a touch perfunctory; they'd never solicit your opinion unless they absolutely had to. Once, you saw them laughing in a huddle in the corridor and the thought crossed your mind that they were saying something about you.

Now their smile is genuine. They are interested in how you see things. They're glad to have you around. When they were under pressure they asked for your help.

One thing that's nice is that you'd built up a slightly forbidding picture of this person – which is now being dismantled. Going on their initial behaviour towards you, you'd imagined them as someone generally severe and cold. But recently they mentioned – out of nowhere – that they're thinking of moving house; they told you they're interested in gardening and would love to have a vegetable patch. And a few days ago they confided that they're worried they might have misjudged the relationship with one of the suppliers or been over-optimistic about the market position in Ireland. They're ready to let you know something a bit vulnerable about themselves. You could use this against them, but they – rightly – realise you won't. You'd only seen one side of them. Actually it turns out they've got some quite sweet sides to them.

And now you don't necessarily hold their earlier wariness against them. They weren't being mean. Their earlier attitude was (you're coming to think) justified caution. You know that you're a perfectly OK person in yourself and that you are pretty competent and devoted – but that doesn't mean it was clear to them. They didn't just want to know about good intentions. They wanted to know if you could actually be relied on in a tricky situation or that you could deliver really good-quality work, or that you'd see the bigger picture or come up with genuinely helpful initiatives on your own. This person's goodwill is worth having because they don't give it away automatically. They have warmed to you because you have proved yourself. Their approval is a measure of your own development. One is being properly judged before being endorsed. Of course we like it when people are warm and positive from the very start. It's tempting to get annoyed because people don't automatically know what we're capable of. But we can actually come to respect when they wait for evidence of that.

'Getting' a Great Work of Art for Yourself

From time to time you've been standing in one of the world's great galleries in front of an acclaimed master-piece. You could see that the work was quite nice or fairly interesting. But not much more than that. It was hard to fathom what all the fuss was about. But you probably kept the thought to yourself. There's so much cultural prestige swirling around art that it's not especially good for the ego to announce to a group of swooning compan-ions – or even to yourself – that you simply don't 'get' the work. Maybe you've forced yourself into to a more cerebral attitude. You've learned from the audio guide that the work in question used to be believed to have been painted in Siena in 1423 but new evidence suggests it may in fact have originated in Florence in 1431, from the hand of an artist trained in Siena (this point is stressed) thus shedding light on the question of the cultural relationship between these cities at that time – an issue that, up to that point, had never greatly troubled you.

One senses that a huge quantity of intellectual labour has been devoted to this darkish, smallish object, and one is naturally reluctant to dismiss it out of hand. Well-informed people seem to be enthused. And here it is, in any case, on display with a spotlight training down on it, in a silk-walled room in a huge and very impressive build-ing. It must be truly wonderful. Only a little rebellious part of one's mind stays loyal to the sceptical thought: but I don't get it.

We're naturally worried about looking foolish or getting something terribly wrong: saying, 'I love Leonardo da Vinci', when this turns out to be by someone completely different whose name hasn't ever crossed our path before; or being bored by a work that's drawn a big crowd and is presumably a highlight of western civilisation, by which it would be embarrassing to be unmoved. And of course there are varied versions of this kind of thing that go on around prominent examples of contemporary art as well. We're informed the artist is interrogating the essence of photography or is a key influence on the Dusseldorf school – which sounds highly impressive in the abstract but doesn't really answer the shy, but persistent, question: why should I care about that?

In contrast to all this, there's the special pleasure of finding that, in fact, the work has an intimate meaning: it speaks to you. The change in experience can happen particularly if we're looking at a postcard or screensaver image – that is, at things officially regarded as mere shadows of the original. But they have a huge advantage. We encounter them in private: we don't feel the world looking over our shoulders, checking up to see if we're getting it right. We can turn to them when the mood takes us; we're not restricted by an external schedule, which tells us we have to make the most of *The Night Watch* or *Guernica* at 11.45 am on Tuesday morning, slightly jet-lagged and jostled by a school tour group, because that's when our travel arrangements happen to land us in front of the masterpiece itself.

Mood is a crucial ingredient in the experience. A work of art has got something it wants to say to us, but we need to be in the right frame of mind to receive it. The mind is a bit like a radio: the waves are coming in all the time but the device needs to be tuned to the right frequency to pick up the programme. It's an unfortunate accident that the big gallery itself can often constrain our moods and natural that a postcard or an image in a book allows that our mood can be more attuned: we can take a look at it when feeling sad or worried about what's happening in a relationship or excited about a new opportunity, a bit wistful or sombre.

In the right mood, you feel close to that person in the picture who looks so sad and yet so dignified; or a bright scattering of paint looks like a joyful, hopeful gesture rather than a puzzling step in the evolution of technique. You can bring yourself into engagement with the work.

Normally, we feel we're supposed to wait for others to tell us what we're supposed to think about a great work of art. We peer at labels and tried to imagine what a friend who studied art history might say. What we're discovering now is a kind of independence. 'Getting it' doesn't mean that you've arrived at the same conclusion as the experts. It means that the work feels important to you in your own life. You might not know the dates or who influenced this artist or whether this was a late or an early work; you couldn't say if this work was typical of the time (which was when exactly? You are a bit hazy) or innovative. But these factors don't seem decisive anymore. Because you've latched onto something more fundamental: the work exists for you.

That's why getting one work of art opens a door to the enjoyment of many others. Because you've discovered in yourself the key to engagement. As with learning to swim or to ride a bike: you don't just master one bicycle or learn how to stay afloat in a single pool – you gain a general confidence that you can take to them all. You have acquired trust in the validity of your own reactions. There is a step away from intimidation: you can find yourself at home around something, or in a place, that used to feel alien.

Very Dark Jokes

It can be disconcerting for a nice person – one who wishes well to others and wants to be kind, reasonable and honourable – to think they may take quiet satisfaction in dark humour. On the face of it we're smirking and giggling and occasionally practically falling out of our chairs with laughter at things which – soberly considered – range from the obnoxious to the horrific. We're tickled by jokes about ...

> *stupidity:* a man encountering a toilet brush which he had, up to that moment, regarded as a fictional object – the domestic equivalent of a UFO.

> *cruelty:* a story about Hitler getting frantic as he falls behind with his to-do list.

> *greed:* three Wall Street bankers walk into a bar ...

> *heartlessness:* there's this boat full of refugees and it springs a leak and ...

> *violence:* a jaunty entry in Jack the Ripper's diary, 'Somewhat tired after long walk last night. Get shoes resoled. Peckish when home. Egg sandwich! Nearly forgot, slashed lady.'

The pleasure that we derive from dark jokes is not really connected – as we may fear – with approval of the things we find amusing. It's actually based on something that – at first – seems surprising: the feeling of closeness to, and connection with, other people. But it makes sense when we keep in mind how intimacy can grow around a shared admission that life is actually far weirder than we normally make out. A crucial ingredient of the pleasure is the idea that we are not simply laughing alone: our laughter is in common with the person telling us the joke and with the other people around us who find it just as funny as we do.

For sensible reasons, our public selves are quite heavily edited portraits of our inner lives. We hate with more vigour than we like to let on and we rightly school ourselves to be rational and to tone this down as far as we can around other people. But the loathing and disgust simmers in the dark. We are much more inadequate in multiple areas than we feel we can afford to reveal to others: horror at the prospect of phoning an acquaintance; a deep disinclination, painfully overcome, to brush one's teeth; zero willpower in the presence of wine/porn/ice cream; inability to stick to the simplest budget; a life-long rage against one's hair or lack of it; a tendency to get enraged by minor domestic affronts. We understandably hesitate to announce these frailties to the world but we're hugely conscious of them and this creates a zone of loneliness. And typically we are more sexually desiring, and more perverse in our desires, than we would ever like to say: we harbour at the back of our minds scenarios that, apparently, no decent person would normally admit to.

All these things can be given a humorous spin using the standard comic devices: incongruity, unexpected emphasis, mockery and droll elaboration. And being funny about them is reassuring. It means the other person, who is making the joke, is on top of the rather combustible material. They can be witty because they've got a lot of distance on the subject. We know for certain they won't actually embrace the thing they are joking about; that's why they are joking. They're not cheering on Jack the Ripper or sympathising with the tricky task of running the Third Reich. A joke isn't a sly way of sketching a plan.

Dark humour at first appears like the enemy of the mature self; it keeps on asking us to find the least admirable parts of human nature entertaining. But its pleasure lies in its kindness: dark humour is inviting us to compassion for ourselves and for others; it teaches the generous, tender idea that the more disturbed parts of our minds are manageable and are, in fact, central to the noblest ideal: that of being able to love others as they truly are.

Midnight Walks

Maybe you should be in bed, but something – you might not know exactly what – is keeping your mind active. You need to extract yourself from home, get away from a screen and get a little distance from whoever else might be around. Maybe it's cold outside and you tie a thick scarf under your chin.

It could be a blissfully warm night – the heat of the day has finally relented; now it's the perfect temperature and you can go for a stroll just in a T-shirt.

You've got the world pretty much to yourself. The street lights are slightly yellow (if they still use the older sodium lamps in your area). It's a deeply familiar, comforting glow. As a child you loved to look at the lights from the back seat of the car as you returned home late from an evening at your grandparents' house. The street lamps are such little things, struggling against the vastness of the dark. It's amazingly hard for the human race to provide even just a tiny fraction of the natural illumination of the day over even only a tiny portion of the earth's surface.

You notice the moon: a lemon-slice shape, silvery-grey, partly obscured by cloud. The sun is shining up there. It looks like an interesting place. You sympathise for a moment with the vast majority of those who have ever lived who imagined the moon inhabited – usually by beings cleverer and kinder than us; such a pity it turned out to be just a lump of rock and dust. It doesn't look all that far away; it's not surprising people thought they could touch it from the top of a tower just a little higher than any they managed to construct.

Things often look nicer at night; irksome details are lost in the shadows. A few lights are on behind curtains and blinds. Occasionally you see into a room on an upper storey: the top of a bookcase, a corner of kitchen ceiling. A cat observes you from the top of a wall. You turn slightly at random down one street then another; it doesn't matter very much where you go.

The pleasure of a midnight walk is often to do with the opportunity it provides for thinking. The late hour, the gentle motion of the body, the well-known yet newly strange streets, our own inner restlessness and the fact of being alone and not having anywhere in particular to get to (except, eventually, home) combine to create a sympathetic environment for the strange operation of the brain we call 'thinking'.

'Thinking' sounds so familiar: in some way or another our brains are active the whole time; but in its more ambitious sense, thinking is the process by which we address and make progress towards resolving a matter which is both important and confusing. Thinking involves seven key phases, and over the course of an ideal midnight walk we would be making our way through them to the accompanying rhythm of our footsteps on the dark pavement.

One: Selection
At any moment there could be many things that are bugging or exciting you: someone has been horrible; the tax return is looming; a news item; you drank too much on Friday and maybe were a bit of an idiot; your mother been prescribed some pills; a new friend; feeling a bit

lonely; the documentary you watched earlier; a slight twinge in your left knee; a new work project; the dream you had last night ... Typically, we jump around between them all. The starting point is to select just one for the midnight walk. The problem isn't finding the right one. They are all important – and with enough walks we'll get round to them all. The first move is just to pick one and to stick with it.

Two: The admission of ignorance

Strangely, a major block in thinking is the tendency to come to a conclusion too quickly. We often start out feeling we know what's going on. Typically, one repeats an assertion in different ways. One feel things like: that person is awful; they did this thing and they also did that thing. They're arrogant; they're mean. They are so full of themselves. The issue is being restated again and again. But we don't actually make progress in thinking. This is why, weirdly, it's such a key step to recognise that often one doesn't know, for instance, what is going on in another person's mind, or what their motives really are, or why they behave as they do. Or when presented with a money worry, one thinks – of course it's about money. It seems so obvious. And yet the real issue might be somewhere else (a feeling of failure, envy, the terror of being humiliated by comparison with a rival, the worry of having wasted one's opportunities). But we can't get to these matters if we're initially convinced we know exactly what the trouble is about.

The fact is, though, that we rarely see more than a few parts of what a person fully is, even though by ordinary standards we know them well. We so quickly forget everyone's complex background. And others don't constantly remind us of the accumulation of shame, compromise, fear and difficult experiences that have shaped them. On the surface they appear sure of themselves or aggressive or enviably fortunate; they let us down or ask too much; they don't listen properly or they laser in on our failings in a humiliating way. Our complaints against others are endless. But at midnight, away from others (except a stray neighbour walking their dog), we can briefly get enough distance to recall the strangeness of being human. We are deeply peculiar organisms; we are mysteries to one another and to ourselves; we don't really know why we ourselves do what we do half the time.

Three: Sympathy for oneself

It would be so sweet if life were trouble-free. We get bothered by the pure fact of having problems – we feel unfairly beset by them, cursed and burdened. Why do these things come my way? In order to understand our problems we have to recognise them as legitimate and, in broad outline, normal.

Life is essentially quite difficult. It's acceptable to have this problem (even if it seems like it's a tiny thing that's on your mind: the electricity bill was larger than I was expecting; I found some more grey hairs; I bought a chair and actually I don't really like it; I said I was going to have to do some extra work on Saturday and my partner looked at me as if it was my fault). In the night it's a little easier to keep in mind that the human condition is sombre; we are frail creatures inhabiting the outer crust of a minuscule lump of rock orbiting a very average star. It is so understandable we have troubles.

Four: Reverie

Ideally, we would then ask ourselves what else comes to mind around the issue we are focusing on. The associations could seem quite odd at first. Maybe the pills make you think of a childhood holiday when your mother played in a tennis tournament and did quite well; or a story she told you about her grandmother (who died quite a number of years before you were born) falling down the stairs at her house in Sheffield and lying at the bottom for four hours before a neighbour who was coming round for lunch got worried and called the police.

Or, the documentary about farmers in Norway and how they cope with the long winter – which was very lovely – makes you think how when you were little you loved a book about two children who went round the world on a magic carpet, stopping for minute or two in lots of countries – and you used to wonder, where will I live? You didn't think you'd end up near Manchester. And it also brings to mind a holiday in Turkey years back (when you thought you might marry your ex) and, bizarrely, something your hairdresser said about liking getting postcards from her clients when they are away.

We're not initially asking for it all to make sense. What we're doing is building up a sense of what this starting point means to us. We're mapping the surrounding emotional terrain. It can seem counter-intuitive. Aren't we meant to be solving a problem, while this just seems to be making everything more murky? The deeper fact, though, is that it is out of this material that we'll grasp what's really getting to us.

Five: Defining the need

As we approach the railway bridge or the shuttered corner shop, we get onto the next phase: so what is it that's really at stake here? The pills might not mean so much; I'm worried about my mother's health (though that's the case) but I feel I haven't come to know her fully and time could be running out. The documentary might have touched me not because I'm especially interested in Norway but because I've always wanted to live by the sea and I wonder what it means if I never do.

Around finances, the key thing might not be this specific squeeze but the fact that I seem to get myself into these situations. Around an annoying partner, the move might be from why are they so touchy to: so why am I really with them? – as an open question, seeking possibly a good, positive answer.

Definition means getting to a question that you can do something about. So often our minds are taken up with assertions: it's grim; she's down on me; he's a creep. But it's really only questions that we can address and ultimately do anything about.

Six: Practical focus

What should I do? I can stick with things as they are, I can maybe abandon the whole issue (leave, quit, resign) or I can try to make some adjustment in myself to improve the situation. I can't pin any hopes on others changing. That would be nice, but it's not directly in my power to bring that about.

Seven: Perspective

Life is short; the universe is big; one occupies for a moment (really) a tiny portion of existence. Usually we like the idea of being noticed and of feeling important. But at other points it is sweet to feel that maybe our actions don't matter – they will be lost in the greater tides of human existence, and all our follies and errors will melt away very soon, as if they had never been. We are off the hook. The night helps this thought come forward. Somewhere across the globe where it is day, people are grabbing lunch or leading their cattle to the waterhole. They know nothing of us and our troubles. Not out of callousness, but because, really, our problems are quite small. Galaxies are very slowly exploding; there are stars being born in labours of tens of millions of years; others are in their billion-year-long death throes. And all it will mean, at most, on earth, is the tiniest fluctuation in the tiniest flicker of light in a minute portion of the night sky. Yet, at the same time, we're not nothing. We are truly marvellous organisations of sensitivity, thought, feeling and longing.

It really is late now. Returning home, you finger the door key – a little calmer, a little more resolute; you yawn at the last corner; at last you're not simply tired, you're beginning to feel sleepy. It's nice to think you'll soon be going to bed. Soon thought will cease; consciousness will be suspended; the sources of energy will be renewed. It is already the very beginning of tomorrow.

Flirtation

There's a person at another firm you quite often have to speak to on the phone – mostly about recurrent issues with a licensing agreement. You've never actually met them (you're in different parts of the world), though their profile photo is intriguing: a crisp shirt, nice glasses – but you know you can't necessarily tell very much from that. It's always fun chatting with them – you like their voice; when there's a problem they spin out a sympathetic phrase 'oh ... I know ... I know' – you're really only lamenting an ambiguity in the clauses about merchandising rights, but their tone suggests other possible occasions when they might say that in the same way: if you told them about feeling lonely at the sales conference in Antwerp or the way Bach's cantata 'Bist du bei mir' sometimes makes you want to cry. They're not saying anything intimate outright, they are just hinting. They are creating a suggestive atmosphere that invites you to join in. You might exaggerate your excitement around banal things ... 'it's so lovely of you to ... have a senior partner clarify the corporate advertising strategy': the way you say it – stressing 'lovely' – implies something bigger: you are lovely. They sign off in a sweet way: 'till soon'. Which conjures up a double-cheek kiss, a sympathetic glance into your eyes and a pat on your arm. It's a charming little flirtatious moment in the middle of a tricky afternoon.

You might find yourself flirting at a party, when you meet up with an old friend, when you have tea with a lovely elderly neighbour, across the boardroom table, with a colleague at work or even with your partner. It's possible to take a negative view of flirting – most often when someone we like flirts with someone other than us. But that's because flirting is understood only in a very narrow way: as an early step in a mating ritual that tests the waters for sex.

But the pleasure of flirting is not primarily erotic. It's more aligned with friendship. And its core impulse is generosity. Essentially, when we flirt we are showing another person that we like them and find them attractive. When people are good at flirting it's clear that they are many steps away from a suggestion of hopping into bed – though there might be a hint that it would be nice to stroke this person's hair, or cuddle them or whisper to them in the dark. But these are pleasures of affection and it's unfortunate if we categorise them mainly as foreplay.

Some people could do with toning down their self-esteem, but usually we're not at all given to overestimating how much other people might be interested in us (the problem typically runs the other way; we find it increasingly difficult to imagine being the object of desire for anyone); we don't need to follow through with this person – the benefit is a needed boost to one's self-perception. And we love it when another person indicates that they think we are just a little bit lovely. We usually need plenty of reminders of this.

One of the nice things about flirting is that it is highly flexible. People can flirt across gulfs of political belief, of social, economic or marital status, of sexual inclination and (with obvious caveats) of age: the 26-year-old corporate lawyer and the 52-year-old man behind the counter of the corner shop can flirt; so can the cleaner and the CEO. And it's moving when they do because they are demonstrating how kindness and interest and a touch of mutual attraction can overcome distance.

Because flirting is non-committal, it can look as if it is insincere. Isn't the flirt only pretending? This is an attitude fostered by a Romantic ideal of total coherence: either we are completely sincere and speak straight from the heart or we are, in effect, liars. So, in some of the great Romantic novels of the nineteenth century, 'flirt' is a term of abuse; the brooding hero would be applauded for renouncing his fiancée (and retiring, in disgust at the world, to a partially ruined castle in the Highlands) if she flirted with another man; and no fine heroine would ever adopt a playful, semi-erotic tone with anyone except her single true love. But they missed something important.

The ideal flirtation is a small work of social art co-created by two people; it is civilised artifice. It acknowledges limitations; it is worried about consequences; it knows you shouldn't let a momentary impulse damage a long-standing relationship. So it invents a safe version of seduction. It constitutes a wise accommodation with reality, while working out how to have the nicest time with another person. We should flirt more.

49

The First Day of Feeling Well Again

It wasn't, hopefully, too serious, just enough to keep you in bed, and feeling a bit miserable, for three or four days: you got a flu virus, you had an unusually heavy cold or a bout of tonsillitis.

Being unwell – obviously – is far from desirable. But all the same it had certain compensations. You had a bowl of lentil soup – hot and bland, you sensed its worthy goodness seeping into you: calming and nutritious. Someone brought you a cup of weak tea and this little act of kindness really touched you. A crunchy, bland slice of dry toast – which normally you'd never consider eating – was very appealing.

While you were feeling poorly, certain themes of your life took a back seat. It didn't seem to matter so much what was happening at work. You didn't have the energy to get roused by the little things that so often irritate you. You took a break from scanning the news. You didn't feel obliged to respond to texts and emails. Your sexual appetites were in recession and stopped occupying your mind. You felt oddly calm. And that tranquillity lingers as you start to feel better.

You slept well last night. Your body is newly functional. Things you'd never normally even notice are sources of positive pleasure. Being able to breathe easily is interesting: how nice to feel the air drawing through the paranasal sinuses; it's lovely to be able to swallow without wincing. You can focus on the back of your head – there's not a trace of the throb that's been your companion for the last 48 hours. Your eyes feel energetic. Your brain is coming alive. Feeling hungry is really very nice. The mere act of standing up (without feeling dizzy or weak) is a pleasure in itself. It's rather fascinating to put on proper clothes, and going outside seems, briefly, like a treat.

As we re-emerge into the world, we are remaking acquaintance with things that had been taken for granted but now seem fascinating. You haven't used a house key for a few days and you see it anew as a beautifully intricate machine that by a process you almost (but don't quite) understand can manoeuvre the small tongue of steel that is the only real barrier between your private domestic civilisation and the barbarian world into its snug little slot. You turn the key this way and that in the lock for the sheer pleasure of hearing the decisive click of closure alternate with the flat thud of release. A shoelace seems astonishing: how odd that we tie ourselves into our shoes with little bits of string and that our culture has very strict ideas about what the knot should be like – theoretically you could knot the ends together 50 times into a large ball and it's curiously tempting to give it a go. One is returned to the condition of a child who has just mastered the art of doing up a zip and for whom zips are still (what they always really are) wondrous little pieces of portable engineering generously sewn into one's clothes for entertainment value.

We're not literally required to be ill to have these pleasures. Potentially we could discover them by the pure exercise of imagination – but mostly we have to wait for the special prompt of a few days lying in bed.

50

Daisies

They're so small: you have to lie down to see them properly in their native state, scattered in small groups or sprouting in isolation in the unmowed grass. They start showing themselves in April and can still be around in October. *Bellis perennis* – the common daisy – can live from year to year (even if a rotor blade does regularly decapitate it), so long as its roots can extract enough moisture from the soil; none, however, are known for certain to have survived more than 20 years, but this may reflect our limited curiosity rather than indicate the natural horizon of their being.

At the height of their flourishing, they may only stand five centimetres tall. The conjunction of the golden yellow of the cluster of tiny heads at the centre and the fringe of just off-white petals is one of nature's most charming colour arrangements: it might make one think for a moment of a fried egg or of the interior of a Russian palace from the time of Catherine the Great.

The primary use humanity has discovered, so far, for this particular flower is the daisy chain. Making daisy chains – you use a thumbnail to make a slit low down on the stem and thread another one through – sounds fiddly, but turns out to be very easy.

During the hours of darkness, the petals fold inwards and close up, and they reopen in the morning (which was the origin of their name: 'day's eye'). It is obvious, today, that the action of the flower is purely mechanical: the petals are actually arranged in two overlapping layers – though this isn't obvious unless you look out for it. When the light levels fall below a particular level, the lower ring of petals grows very slightly faster than the upper one and, because of the intricate way the petals are interleaved, this causes the whole head to close. But it is unsurprising that to earlier, more imaginative, ages this nightly ritual implied obscure impulses of exhaustion or lamentation; the daisy was sleeping or possibly mourning the absence of its lover, the sun. It was a benign misconception, suggesting a spiritual affinity of man and plant.

But, still, we can see the daisy as subject – like us – to a daily rhythm. It's not specifically the degree of ambient light that regulates our behaviour, but external, biological factors dominate our lives as well, though we typically resist the assertion that they do. We don't like to think that we might be upset by a colleague in part because it is raining and cold or that our feeling that a relationship is on the ropes may be in large part due to the fact that we're tired. We usually reserve these generous insights for babies, whose darker moods we readily assign to hunger or being too hot or needing a sleep. In a slightly wiser world, one might think as one's partner turns sour over a trivial matter: 'It's Sunday evening, their emotional petals are closing.'

Once we actually pay them proper attention, daisies are not only beautiful and charming in themselves. They also provide an unexpected, yet telling, point of access to a major cultural issue: the imperfect distribution of cultural prestige. Because – in spite of how nice they really are – daisies are not taken seriously.

You can't actually buy an ordinary daisy. The nearest you can get is ordering a packet of daisy seeds or (at an extreme) buying a house with daisies growing on the lawn. But you don't see them in florists' shops and

Interflora don't deliver them. We don't give each other bunches of daisies to mark special occasions. We don't go for special trips to look at famous daisy gardens. Couples don't purchase a single daisy as a token of their love. This isn't really evidence of any failure on the part of this particular flower. Rather, it's an oversight on our part. We disdain the daisy for an unfortunate reason: it is abundant. It's a victim of the unfortunate idea that to be special something has to be rare. Prestige is the current collective list of what is worthy of attention – the public guide to what might be enjoyable or nice; but it isn't necessarily as yet complete.

Small, pretty and very common, the daisy is (amongst other good things) a guide to the ideal economy of the future.

51

Figs

Every so often, you encounter a fig. It might turn up as a decorative aside to a dessert at a smart restaurant you occasionally go to when you want to mark a special occasion; from a couple of years back you remember there were baskets of them in the market in Cadiz which caught your eye, but you couldn't pluck up the courage to join the bustle at the stall and actually buy some; your sister puts them in the adventurous salads she sometimes serves; and they're in the supermarket somewhere but you're usually in hyperfocused mode there and race as fast as possible to the things you always buy.

Between these sporadic meetings, you don't think much about figs at all. Their existence is just one of a billion facts of which you are peripherally, passively aware.

But when a fig does come your way, you are always rather charmed. The colours inside are lovely, of course. And the slightly dry texture of the flesh and its quiet taste are pleasant. You like figs, you remind yourself. And then it might be half a year before another lands in front of you on a plate. You're hardly even sure when their season is (do they even have one?).

It's a curious type of situation: there's a small pleasure we have, but we leave having it very much to chance. And even when we do have the opportunity, often a lot of other things get in the way: the conversation takes a lively turn; your little nephew starts to wail in his bassinet; the combination is a bit unfortunate (the cacao bean chocolate was very nice but it annihilated the figs).

To work against this randomness, we need to invoke an idea that initially can sound a bit remote: ritual. We might initially associate ritual with archaic ceremonies, such as a coronation, or with cultish gatherings. But there are more helpful images: the tiny ritual of blowing out the candles on a birthday cake and making a wish before cutting the first slice – slightly garbled traces of rather nice ideas: a birthday marks the end of one year of life and the beginning of the next; we should ideally focus our minds on transience and hope. And maybe the ritual was once more explicitly geared to helping us do this.

When we boil it down to its essence, the point of a ritual is to mandate a set of actions and attitudes in order to get us into a valuable state of mind. It is – like a recipe – a set of rules that, if we follow them carefully, will bring about a certain result; not in this case a bowl of watercress soup or a crème brûlée, but, rather, a state of heightened appreciation. Unlike a recipe, a ritual usually comes with instructions about when you have to do it. Recipes leave it up to us – when you happen to feel like making a risotto, here's what to do. But a ritual includes directions about when you should do it – every 365 days after your birth, when the new moon rises or when the cherry or plum trees are in blossom (as with Hanami, ritualised picnics in Japan devoted to an appreciation of the transience of natural beauty). The ritual comes with a date; it makes an appointment in your diary, placed there by your culture. The ritual is rightly worried we'll forget to pursue a particular pleasure – so it comes with a reminder.

Often with a ritual, the details have been honed and re-fined over a long period of time. People have thought quite hard how to get the most out of what they were doing. Rituals frequently invite us to quite specific patterns of thought and action. The Jicarilla Apache of New

Mexico, for example, have an elaborate ceremony for adolescent girls which lasts for several days, The girls must wear special costumes and must pay close attention to particular stories and songs – designed to foreground a range of admirable qualities. The ritual is hugely ambitious because it aims to transform how they think about themselves and how they see their place in society.

If we were to invent a ritual around appreciation of the fig, it could go like this:

Every Tuesday, after work, we'll pick up some figs from the grocery opposite the train station. Place the fig on a plain white plate the first few times – the better to concentrate on the delicate, cool green hues of the skin. Later you can experiment with another background: celadon or maybe black. Before you do anything else, take a moment to contemplate the essential strangeness of this small fruit. It could have evolved more like an acorn: highly effective from the point of view of propagation, but alien to the human system. It could have been more like the strawberry – so sweet and obviously charming as to be already utterly familiar. The fig, at this moment, is our point of entry.

With a very sharp knife, cut it into quarters, lengthwise. The need for sharpness doesn't arise from hardness but because they are soft; blunt pressure would spoil them. The edges of the pieces should be clean and the inner surface perfectly flat. Look at the tints and hues of the flesh. For 15 seconds, imagine you are a painter, trying to portray the pattern: make your eyes stick with it.

Think of the tree it came from. This particular piece of fruit might have ripened in a plastic tunnel outside Basingstoke, but its ancestors flourished in historic times in Palestine or in Sicily and figured in the parables of tribes.

Squeeze a few drops of lemon onto the sliced flesh – some will miss (it's hard to aim with a lemon). This will intensify the flavour. Finally, take a bite. Concentrate first on the texture. Then, with a second bite, focus on the taste. The ritual of the fig should last about seven minutes.

The ritual reminds us what to do in order to have a nicer time. It operates with a benign idea of rules and regulations. They're not, in this case, to stop us doing something that might be rather convenient at this moment. Instead, they guide us to having a better time. This approach to rules is a revision of the Romantic ideal of spontaneity, the lucky moment, which is excited by ideas of happy accidents and chance encounters. It's not that these are always terrible ideas at all. It's just that they aren't the only template we need. If we only follow them, a lot of good things won't happen, or will happen only very rarely, when your sister just happens to take it into her head to ask you round to lunch.

Small pleasures need rituals. The irony (as it were) of the small pleasure is that it isn't intense enough usually to force itself upon us – we don't become addicted or obsessed; the pull is much weaker than that of sex or video games or drinking wine or wolfing down a bar of chocolate; these are pleasures we need no reminding of, and we often have to painfully struggle to limit their sway in our lives. With small pleasures it's the opposite. We're more likely to lose touch with them. They easily get crowded out. We actively need to build up their presence in our lives.

A List of Very Small Pleasures

Once we're on the lookout for them, life seems filled with small pleasures. The point isn't simply to note them but to understand why we like them – which intensifies and deepens the satisfaction they offer. And then to make a more reliable, larger place for them in our lives.

One

Tidying a cupboard: a bounded task, you can get it absolutely right – while most things in life are a bit of a fudge; pleasant busyness when there's no real hurry; pride in being fussy about little details; don't necessarily tell anyone; you are doing it for yourself; lovely when it's done: a tiny part of life is now solved; pop back later to admire your creation.

Two

Borrowing a friend's scarf: it doesn't quite suit; by wearing it you are making a statement; nicely intimate; being part of a team of two; sweetly hesitant foreplay: 'it's so cold … you know, you could borrow a scarf … if you want to'; look at it in the cupboard and think nice thoughts about its real owner; ideally you are always going to return it but never quite do – and they're secretly pleased.

Three

Aphorisms: nicely compact, portable; the pleasure of summing up; they are always a bit wrong if you push them too hard; but you don't mind; on the lookout for a chance to use them; this bit of wisdom is now yours.

Four

Memorising a line of poetry: 'If I should die, think only this of me …'; 'and all shall be well, all manner of things shall be well'; 'If I had world enough and time …'; hard to get the rhythm perfect; don't worry about what comes next; your own thoughts build around it; occasionally reveal one, shyly, to a friend, though it will never mean quite to them what it means to you.

Five

Saying 'fuck' (if you usually don't): you're tougher than you supposed; sometimes for the sheer drama of surprising people (did they really just say 'fuck'?); very nice when praising a refined merit ('so fucking noble and tender'); cathartic when you drop a saucepan on your toe ('oh fuck'); the less you swear the more enjoyable a good 'fuck' gets.

Six

Sharpening a pencil: metal pencil sharpener; changeable blade (though you have never changed it); finding the perfect balance between forward pressure and rotation; the simplest machine – impossible to improve; not too sharp, so the lead gouges the paper or snaps off.

Seven

Picnics in odd places: on a tiny roof garden surrounded by tomato plants; sheltering behind a rock on a windy winter's day by the sea; in a tree house; on the kitchen floor. A familiar thing in a new place; mutual revelation.

Eight

Celadon blue: or perhaps it is really a shade of green; hard to decide; it's serene without being passive; cool and ample – your gaze can rest in it; quiet; best for small, curved things – a bowl, a vase, a pair of socks; lovely against white.

Nine

Learning how to forgive: the pain could be from years back – the bully, the bastard, the bitch who hurt you; outwardly you said it didn't matter anymore, but you still hated them; forgiveness isn't just forgetting, it's reimagining the person who wounded you; they had their troubles surely, however well they hid them, though you may never know what they were; they lashed out because they were lashed at by someone or something; you're cleaner, more relaxed as bitterness melts away.

Ten

The extraordinary heat as you walk down the plane steps: it's physical, in your lungs, pressing on your forehead; it warms the muscles deep in the shoulders; it implies awnings, big rotating fans on the ceiling, sunglasses, pale garments worn loose, afternoon naps, lemons, ice; the whole idea of climate strikes you; you're going to be someone slightly different here; it's the birth of your tropical twin; a twinge of pity for the self who lived so long in the cold.

Eleven

Thick socks: worn indoors, after a bath or a bruising day at work; you're hardly ever nice to your feet or ankles – they've been promoted; the toes are free yet cosy; it helps with everything – you respond patiently to an inconvenient request, you listen more carefully when your partner tells you something; you feel sensual without the inconvenient clamour of sexual desire; they were on sale at £4.99; so much for so little.

Twelve

Being offered the kind of biscuit you liked as a child: it's been years, you only had them when you were quite little; one time you went into the kitchen very early in the morning and took a handful back to bed with you; you liked to pull them apart and eat them from the inside out; you liked licking them, you could eat them just with a million licks; you take a nibble; it's not as nice as you'd remembered, your palate has changed; but you liked the little you who liked them so much; you wish you could give them one now.

Thirteen

Building sites: it's messy, but everything has a very definite purpose and reason for being there; they are the ingredients of an extension or a new block of flats; the pile of bricks will eventually be sorted into a wall against which one day a chemical engineer will place a prized side table bargained for proudly in halting French in a flea market in Bordeaux; the machines are so carefully contrived, the different scoop heads for gouging trenches; the pools of muddy clay will be landscaped away; people will welcome their friends at a door that's currently on order from a supplier in Wolverhampton; it looks like chaos now, but the builders have been through this a million times, and they can already clearly see the end.

Fourteen

After exercise: tough when you were doing it; now you're the virtuous person who has just exercised; the pleasing ache in the limbs to prove your efforts were real; it seems so logical – you suffer and the outcome is good; the will demands and the body obeys, eventually; we're glimpsing the ideal structure of the rest of life.

Fifteen

Intelligent eyes: it's such a big, nebulous concept – intelligence takes so many forms; at its best, it's wisdom – the ability to understand other people and oneself; you see it in the way they hold your gaze when you get to a tricky moment; how they narrow in accurate scepticism or glint with sympathy when others feel awkward; the desire to be like that.

Sixteen
Lying in a field, looking up: the sky is so far away; a cloud drifts by; how come one never looked properly at the sky before: you can't see where it starts; so beautiful, always there; the normal preoccupations fade; you're no longer an employee, a rate payer, a swing voter, a moderately frustrated lover – you are a child of the universe, a sky gazer, an essential human being undefined; you could look at it forever, except there's a pebble between your shoulder blades and a beetle crawling inside your collar.

Seventeen
A brief burst of righteous anger: the energy, the sudden confidence; you turn on them; normally you try to be peaceable, see the other person's point of view – but sometimes fury works; you're accessing a usually dormant part of the psyche; nice to know you can; it gives dignity to your niceness; you're not polite out of weakness but out of knowledge of your strength; you mostly velvet your paws because you have sharp claws; good that others understand this too.

Eighteen
Rediscovering a nice side of a friend/lover: we've known them so well and so long; the irritants start to predominate; then they do or say something that reminds you so much why you loved them in the first place; the way they overuse a word, a flick of the hair they don't realise they do; a detail uncovers a lost, very charming part of who they are; and the tenderness comes flooding back; why did we ever forget; can we keep hold of it from now on?

Nineteen
Getting the giggles in adulthood: half a laugh, half sheer delight at the glorious, unthreatening absurdity of life;

you giggled your way through being 9 (thanks to Aditya and Jennifer); there was that time when you were 14 and nearly fell off your stool in the chemistry lab, you could hardly hold it in; doesn't happen so much these days (absurdity doesn't usually strike you as charming); lovely when it happens; it means: people are nuts and I don't mind; wisdom breaking through.

Twenty
Understanding a new bit of yourself: you assumed you knew yourself; your hopes and fears seemed constant unchangeable companions; maybe the circumstances are shifting – you're in a new place, a new job, with someone a bit different, learning a new language – and you realise there's more to you than you'd thought; can be disconcerting at first – how is this going to fit with the rest of what's there; and then the open question: if this is me, what else might I find if I learn how to look?

Twenty-one
Clouds: we know all about them, in the abstract, but rarely pass two unbroken minutes just looking at them; their movement is almost always just slightly slower than our attention span allows for; incredible grandeur at times – the chariots of the gods; sometimes puffy, sweet things seeking friends; all the time we're not looking around the world a billion psychodramas are being enacted in the sky; briefly the ego forgets itself.

Twenty-two
A glass of water when you are thirsty: instant relief, suddenly water is magnificent; too much and one is bloated, drowning; it's the need that makes the pleasure; the body sends the clearest most urgent signals, yet the solution is so simple; if only one could do this with other things.

Twenty-three

Thinking someone you don't know looks kind: you don't in fact know anything about them for sure; the way they smile generally at the world; the way they pat someone's arm – as if they mean something important; you sense they know all about grief and have turned it into sympathy; they sense the hidden struggle of every life; they are slow to take offence, because they understand how harassed others get; they know how much a little consideration or courtesy can achieve; they don't resent.

Twenty-four

Flowers in a window box: someone planted them and watched them grow; they love them; they got the seeds online, after pondering a catalogue; they water them from a teapot before heading off to work, a few drops splashing down to the pavement; they wanted a garden, but reality intervened; started as a compromise, now it's a joy; speaks to the imagination; where could I try my version of this? A new box in my life for my equivalent of flowers.

Twenty-five

Changing your mind: it's not so easy to say you were wrong before, but it's nice when you do; you weren't really an idiot before, just a less developed version of you; this is progress; ideally you'll always remember what it was like to be on the other side, like all the best teachers; those you used to disagree with turn out not to be so bad – a rare moment when we actually catch ourselves growing; and it could happen again.

Twenty-six

Dolls' houses: you can see all the rooms at the same time; everything is so easy, you are in control, you can flip a sofa with your finger, move the bath into a bedroom on a whim; lovely to peer into the back and imagine being in there; one is finding out what a home can be – the least childish thing.

Twenty-seven
The national anthems of other countries: one feels, briefly, how nice it would be to be proud to belong to another society; the more grandiose and assertive the music, the better; hopefully with a sad section recalling some collective sorrow which binds the nation together, but of which you know nothing.

Twenty-eight
String: it looks so useful, even though you never do use it; special delight in cutting it with sharp scissors; brown is slightly nicer than white; coil it round your index finger.

Twenty-nine
The Singapore Straits, seen from 25,000 feet as the plane descends at night: the majesty of human achievement, regarded from the right distance; you hum 'We are the champions of the world', very, very quietly to yourself.

Thirty
At the dry-cleaners: the special machines for pressing the arms of jackets; you don't actually know what 'dry' means, an attractive mystery because the answer doesn't matter; you never see them actually doing the cleaning, you only see the results; why stop with clothes, could you dry-clean me?

Thirty-one
Heavy rain: best when rare; by choice at dusk, you're outside but not far from home; even with an umbrella you are going to get soaked; the raindrops really do bounce up off the pavement; you'll have a bath, change early into your pyjamas and a big jumper; the evening is going to be cosy.

Thirty-two

Bestsellers in the window of a foreign bookshop: the titles (*Edin den v Dreven Rim*; *Noli Me Tangere*) look more impressive than those at home, though you don't in fact know what they mean; you have no mental picture of the kind of people who might read them; no envy at not having written them yourself.

Thirty-three

Shadows: wild associations: the shadow of a pot plant looks like a wolf; stretching ahead on the pavement you are impossibly elongated and stubby, your head ripples up the side of a house as you approach; detail is suppressed, you notice outlines; every shadow has much in common; the shadow of a tycoon, a beggar, yourself.

Thirty-four

Gentle motion: the higher branches of trees swaying in a light breeze; a flag fluttering; waves lapping on a lake shore; a train pulling out of a station; someone dancing in perfect time, but only with their shoulders and hips; a slow-motion film of a cheetah running: the idea of grace.

Thirty-five

Letting a young child win a game: it's crucial, of course, that they don't realise; make a string of minor strategic errors so that no particular mistake stands out; if you nearly win, their victory is sweeter; the reward – their glee when an adult proves no match for them; life is full of disappointment, it's nice to be able to buck the trend.

Thirty-six

A child's plans to improve the world: build cities out of Lego (it would be fun); make grown-ups go to bed at the same time as children (so they don't get grumpy); everyone should get a turn at being the king or the president (to make things fair); they don't understand the practicalities so emotional intuition gets more scope: unhappiness is the problem they want to solve – that's a sweet and maybe a wise starting point too.

Thirty-seven
A perfectly packed suitcase: everything, for the moment, is beautifully neat and ordered; it's the ideal number of socks – not too many, nor too few; one smart jacket well folded; the compact hygiene essentials (including a mini tube of toothpaste); more of life should be like this.

Thirty-eight
Fresh French bread, butter: so simple, so reliably delicious; it's the marriage that's magical – the butter is salty and sleek (and pleasantly chill in the mouth), the bread is soft, yet chewy and filling; try to get a bit of crust each bite; puts to shame our complex schemes of enjoyment.

Thirty-nine
Moderately difficult jigsaws: not to be despised; however initially baffling, every piece will definitely fall into place; a very clear and definite sense of having finished, when mostly in life we never truly bring anything to its perfect end; a closed task in a world of open-ended problems; wonderfully completable.

Forty
The sound of cicadas: the ideal sound of midsummer, a hot day; work means making a salad for lunch, driving to glance at a ruined temple and going for a swim in the afternoon; dinner on the patio; pleasant speculations: where are they exactly? How do you pronounce the name? Maybe they're so loud because they're a bit deaf? After a while close the window or go indoors; too much and it drives you nuts.

Forty-one

TV dinner: pasta or rice, sushi – something you don't have to cut up; if there's a boring bit you can get up and make a pot of tea or pour a glass of wine; action drama on the screen, car chases, people stranded on ice floes, titanic power struggles; you are ensconced on the sofa, taking a spoonful of chocolate mousse; not too often or it stops being a treat.

Forty-two

The moment you know a film will be good: a line of dialogue, the way an actor laughs, the elegance of an interior shot; a character you identify with gets into trouble; you start feeling involved ... and it's still only beginning.

Forty-three

Cradling someone: their neck in the crook of your arm, their weight in your lap; you stroke their hair; your touch comforts them; you can make another person feel safe; you can hold them in their troubles; the love you received when you were cradled is returned, or passed on.

Forty-four

Watching people walk about in the streets from five storeys up: the usual details are lost to view: you can't see if someone is good-looking; ages become indistinct – a person is oldish, youngish; you notice how people walk; someone in a red jacket becomes the most famous person in the street; up here one feels tolerant and kindly; everyone is interesting – it's very unlikely anyone will notice you, if you are just standing at the window.

Forty-five

Nice bits of a religion you don't believe in: at one point in a service everyone publicly admits they have failed another person (though they don't have to say who); they think it is important that their places of worship should be very beautiful; lighting a candle in front of a picture of a very sad-looking woman and a child; processions; carrying a book on a silken cushion; ritual bathing; they sing together, quite loudly and very seriously.

Forty-six
Finding the right word: succulent, neatfreak, sombre, sapiosexual, dignified, ambivalent, lucid; pinpoints an experience; deft assistance in getting others to understand what's bothering or exciting us; the dream of articulacy.

Forty-seven
Shared sorrows: you know this too; a moment of closeness; we keep forgetting the shared comfort; not trying to solve the problem; acknowledging the validity of grief; I am with you, when you're down; chipping away at loneliness.

Forty-eight
A new friend: you've not known them long, but they know you well; you learn to see the world through their eyes, diminishing the zones of fear; they teach you their enthusiasm, extending the range of admiration; you get to know the area where they live; finding a new, or old but lost, part of yourself.

Forty-nine
Libraries at dusk: most people have gone home; long series of dulled spines; angled light, last rays through the big windows; lingering motes in the air; a golden pool of concentration under a small reading lamp; serene, cosy; wisdom feels accessible.

Fifty
A long journey in an empty train carriage: peace in a place that's meant to be crowded; deserted platforms; the outskirts of industrial towns; hills in the distance – you look

up again, they've gone; time to think; spreading papers over adjacent seats; going to the loo as the train sways round a bend; might only happen once in your life.

Fifty-one

Untranslatable words: *cafuné* (Brazilian Portuguese) – the act of running one's fingers, gently but deeply, through someone else's hair; *eudaimonia* (Ancient Greek) – the long-term condition of living a good and flourishing life, which includes a full share of frustration, disappointment, loss and suffering – you can possess *eudaimonia* even when you're not feeling very happy at the moment; *age-otori* (Japanese) – to look worse after a haircut; the unfamiliar name makes the idea clearer; another culture understands a part of you.

Fifty-two

Becoming a person who is alive to small pleasures: life has its endless pains and sorrows, but so often there is also something charming and sweet to be appreciated; you don't depend on the endorsement of others – though that would be nice.

Epilogue

The Ideology of Small Pleasures

One: What Is a Small Pleasure?

The normal attitude to small pleasures is to think that they are, individually, perfectly nice but that they are rather insignificant. They come at random into our lives. We savour them for a moment, and then they're gone. We might once in a while mention one of them to someone else. And they might admit that they quite like the sound of rain on a corrugated iron roof or celadon blue or the crumbling wall near the station. But it doesn't go any further. These are small pleasures not so much because the quantity of satisfaction they yield is small – in fact, they may compare well with supposedly big pleasures (being applauded in public, drinking champagne, buying new clothes, staying in a hotel room with a view of the Eiffel Tower).

A pleasure is small in another way: it occupies a small place in our vision of ourselves and of the kind of life we are trying to lead. If asked about what was so nice about a holiday, we don't instinctively reach for things like how we gazed at a cloud for five minutes, how interesting we find scanning machines in airports or how nice it was when our 6-year-old told us about their dream adult life (a premier league footballer who lives at home and stacks shelves in a supermarket quite a lot), though in truth these may have been revealed as the highlights by a pleasureometer strapped discreetly to one's thigh. Whereas the device could well reveal that the official pleasures of the trip (as described by travel brochures, and which we politely reprise in conversation) – seeing coconut trees near white sand, visiting the bazaar and watching local artisans whittle traditional flutes out of marsh reeds – moved us much less.

Small pleasures are the things we enjoy which are currently underrated by what might be called our collective ideology. That is, the elaborately constructed, inherited vision of how to live that has come, through familiarity and the endless prompts of peer pressure, to feel instinctive and natural.

Two: Small Pleasures and Culture

Our culture continues to adopt an attitude to enjoyment which was developed mainly between 1750 and 1900 in Europe and America by poets, artists and novelists who can be grouped together as Romantics. The Romantic idea of enjoyment is deeply impressed by things that are rare, hard to access and which are often connected to travelling far from where one normally lives; Romantics developed a cult of the exotic. They prized the unique moment and were disdainful of repetition. And they tended to be reluctant to explain their enjoyments. They were highly successful publicists and they led people to overlook sources of satisfaction that might be ready to hand; they made it feel a bit strange to try to explain why you like something (preferring that it be mysterious); they encouraged the view that things everyone finds quite nice can't be significant.

A small pleasure can be defined as a pleasure that doesn't fit the Romantic template and therefore seems unimportant. It looks small when regarded in terms of the dominant Romantic ideology: if anyone can have it, if it's easy to come by at home, if it's a pleasure that's best repeated, then it can't be important. Yet the fact is, many of the things that do give us satisfaction have just this character.

At any stage of history a culture may be negligent – it may be generally preoccupied only with a limited range of experiences that it teaches us to look to for satisfaction and fulfilment. The loudest voices in a culture – the most popular songs and games, the most conspicuous adverts, the funniest comedians, the biggest celebrities – may actually never have told us anything much about a whole range of things that can be sweet, delightful, moving or charming. We may very well grow up fully alive to the very real pleasures of fine dining, attending the Olympic opening ceremony or of flying business class: even if we never experience them ourselves, our culture has ensured that we will know all about them. We're primed to recognise the attractions of Venice but less educated in the ways a stroll to the park might be just as nice.

Small pleasures are crucial ingredients in a better existence. What they share is that they tend to be readily available. They don't depend on the deployment of large resources; they are not rare or specialised; they don't require that we make big, effortful adjustments to our lives. Instead, the obstacles to their enjoyment are strangely simple: we don't think about them enough; we don't get much encouragement to focus on them; we don't get reliably reminded of their worth.

A culture isn't only made up of its loud voices. We are not merely passive recipients. We are also, in modest ways, the makers of our collective vision of what is worth paying attention to; we are all in little ways helping each other map the terrain of pleasure more or less accurately. By sharing our own small pleasures with others, we are assisting in the general work of sensitisation – we are making a resource of happiness a little bit more conspicuous. Ideally, when telling another of what we like, we don't just name it, we don't just say 'I like the sound of heavy rain' or 'I love the scent of figs', we go into detail. We try to capture a little more of what it is about these things that we like so much; we try to remember what this made us think of, how we felt, and try to understand why it touched us so deeply. And when another person mentions some little thing that's brought them pleasure, we'd ideally not just nod in agreement but edge them towards a fuller revelation.

Three: Small Pleasures as Therapy

To understand the value of a pleasure to us, we need to look at the contribution it makes to our lives. And that means seeing its therapeutic potential – because 'therapy' is just the general name for psychological help. Anything, including a pleasure, is good because it helps us address our problems or strengthens our virtues. Any particular small pleasure can be linked to one or more of seven key therapeutic moves:

Remembering

We forget things that are important to us; small pleasures are often reminding us of things that are important, but which tend to slip from view.
- Grandmothers
- Feeling at home in the sea
- The song we want to listen to again and again

Hope

We easily slide into cynicism and despair but need hope in order to face important things; small pleasures are often connected to the bolstering of hope.
- Planning the ideal routine
- Looking out from a fifth-floor window
- Up at dawn
- Pleasant exhaustion after a productive day

Dignity of suffering

The problem: suffering is inevitable, but it's linked to panic and desperation; some small pleasures help us cope better with our sorrows – they give the sorrow a more dignified meaning.

- Shared sorrows
- Cows
- Self-pity
- Indulgent pessimism

Rebalancing

The problem is we get unbalanced, and we develop in skewed ways, so important parts of ourselves get neglected.

- Sunday morning
- The desert
- Sunbathing
- Children's drawings

Self-understanding

We are obscure to ourselves and misunderstand what's going on in us (who we are in some key areas of life – in relationships and work); some small pleasures occur around an increase of self-understanding (they are insights into ourselves, wrapped up as pleasures).

- Being teased by old friends
- The fish shop
- A night alone in a hotel
- Crushes

Growth

The problem is that we get stuck with our fears, which are the legacy of bad experiences; these get in the way of potentially better, more mature versions of ourselves; some small pleasures are moments where we're getting a hint about growth.

- Gaining the confidence of a previously suspicious colleague

- 'Getting' a work of art for yourself
- Very dark jokes
- Finding one's feet in another country
- Walks at midnight

Appreciation
The problem: we skate over and glance past things that have much to offer us.
- Grandmothers
- Crying cathartically over the death of a fictional character
- Perhaps all small pleasures fit in this category

Four: Small Pleasures and Capitalism

At various points in the past, charming little things have come into focus and been taken up by the commercial forces of the world and turned into universal and easily recognised pleasures. The idea of eating little bits of pasta twisted into spirals must once have seemed very strange and hard to take seriously; if you had to make your own, almost no one would ever eat them. But they've been taken up by industrialists and advertisers and recipe books and television chefs, and millions of packets of fusilli are now sold in supermarkets every week around the planet. The leading manufacturer, the Barilla Group, has an annual turnover of 3.3 billion euros.

In Japan, much attention is paid to the blossoming of cherry trees. Almost everyone makes a special trip to see them at their best and take special picnics to eat under the white flowers. The boost to the economy is the equivalent of around a trillion yen (around £6 billion). The UK has very nice cherry trees too, but as yet has not developed a portion of the economy around them. And the consequence is that though people in Skegness and Taunton like cherry trees, they don't pay special attention to them and most people find the season has passed before they quite noticed. Building a pleasure into the economy isn't a good thing primarily because it can make money. The argument is rather different. It's that when an industry gets organised, it raises the status of a pleasure and therefore brings it more reliably and impressively to our notice.

There are so many small pleasures whose potential has not yet been fully grasped by society at large – walking at midnight, looking at moss growing on old walls, having a proper conversation with a stranger ...

The idea that these pleasures might sponsor large industries devoted to promoting them sounds odd only because they are not as yet established. The activities in themselves are no less pleasurable than sliding down the side of a mountain (the global skiing industry contributes 60 billion US dollars to the world economy each year) or watching people hit a small ball over a net (the tennis market is 1.5 billion US dollars a year). And of course, a few decades ago a prediction that these enjoyments would flourish on such a scale would have seemed absurd. There are vast industries waiting to emerge around all the things we could enjoy, and benefit from, but don't as yet because we are not systematically encouraged to pay attention to their charms.

**

Small pleasures seem small until we pay them greater and more systematic attention. We are trying to educate ourselves in a central part of life: that of discovering how to make the most of the opportunities for satisfaction that come our way and through them to create for ourselves and others more flourishing and less pained and lonely lives.

Credits

p. 168   TV Mouth, Sheona Beaumont,
          https://www.flickr.com/photos/shospace/5038198233

p. 172   It Is To Laugh, Ed Schipul,
          https://www.flickr.com/photos/eschipul/199259734

p. 176   Let Flowers Speak, Angela Marie Henriette,
          https://www.flickr.com/photos/mara_earthlight/6875448025

p. 180   Dannielle Blumenthal,
          https://www.flickr.com/photos/dannielleblumenthal613/15857265681

p. 192   Faces, Oran Viriyincy,
          https://www.flickr.com/photos/viriyincy/6121304327

p. 204   Bubbles Bubbles Everywhere, Katerina Hlavata
          https://www.flickr.com/photos/kachnch/15873129396

p. 208   The Only Way Is Up, Anders Lejczak,
          https://www.flickr.com/photos/polycola/19107706842

p. 212   Daisies, Jolly Janner,
          https://www.flickr.com/photos/34527231@N06/3450822975

Images courtesy of Flickr, reproduced under Creative Commons License 0, 1.0:

p. 84   Psyche Revived by Cupid's Kiss, by Antonio Canova, 1787, Louvre
          Museum. Joe deSousa,
          https://www.flickr.com/photos/mustangjoe/5841945333

Images courtesy of Marcia Mihotich:

          p. 32; p. 72; p. 88; p. 108; p. 148; p. 152; p. 216.

**Image courtesy of Freenaturestock.com reproduced under Creative Commons
License 0:**

p. 18   Adrian Pelletier,
          http://freenaturestock.com/post/127746705034

Image courtesy of Stokpic.com reproduced under Creative Commons License 0:

p. 40   Lovers Holding Hands On Beach with Bikini, photo by: Ed Gregory,
          http://stokpic.com/project/lovers-holding-hands-on-beach-with-bikini

Images courtesy of Pexels.com, reproduced under Creative Commons License 0:

p. 80   Katie Salerno, Pexels.com,
          https://www.pexels.com/photo/love-people-kissing-romance-18397

p. 132   Bob Clark, Pexels.com,
          https://www.pexels.com/photo/vinyl-music-play-spinning-21148

Image courtesy of Kaboompics.com:

p. 92   Man Reading Newspaper, photo by Kaboompics.com,
          http://kaboompics.com/one_foto/564/man-reading-newspaper

Image courtesy of Tookapic.com:

p. 184   Last Fitting, ©Tookapic.com/Michael Kulesza,
          https://stock.tookapic.com/photos/29003

Images courtesy of Shutterstock.com:

p. 22   Senior woman viewing photo album in living room,
          © Kristo-Gothard Huno, Shutterstock

p. 128   Color magazines in leather living room,
          © Federico Rostagno, Shutterstock

p. 160   Typical Tuscan countryside with cypress and meadow,
          © Zoom Team, Shutterstock

p. 164   Lagoon Nebula, M8, © Igor Chekalin, Shutterstock

p. 188   Two vintage picture frames on wall in art museum,
          with crowd of visitors in blurred motion in background,
          © Amy Johansson, Shutterstock.

Images courtesy of Unsplash.com, reproduced under Creative Commons License 0:

p. 52   Thong Vo,
          https://unsplash.com/photos/Maf7wdHCmvo

p. 76   Eutah Mizushima,
          https://unsplash.com/photos/2TlAsvhqiL0

p. 196   Gabriel Santiago,
          https://unsplash.com/photos/1vYkQVDWXl0

p. 222   Lukasz Szmigiel,
          https://unsplash.com/photos/Hez3-whPnNA

The School of Life is dedicated to developing emotional intelligence – believing that our most persistent problems are created by a lack of self-understanding, compassion and communication. We operate from ten physical campuses around the world, including London, Amsterdam, Seoul and Melbourne. We produce films, run classes, offer therapy and make a range of psychological products. **The School of Life Press** publishes books on the most important issues of emotional life. Our titles are designed to entertain, educate, console and transform.

THESCHOOLOFLIFE.COM